ISSUES THAT CONCERN YOU

Downloading Music

Other books in the Issues That Concern You series:

ISSUES THAT CONCERN YOU

Downloading Music

Linda Aksomitis, *Book Editor*

Christine Nasso, *Publisher*
Elizabeth Des Chenes, *Managing Editor*

GREENHAVEN PRESS

An imprint of Thomson Gale, a part of The Thomson Corporation

THOMSON
™
GALE

Detroit • New York • San Francisco • New Haven, Conn. • Waterville, Maine • London

LIBRARY OF CONGRESS CATALOGING-IN-PUBLICATION DATA

Downloading music / Linda Aksomitis, book editor.
    p. cm. -- (Issues that concern you)
  Includes bibliographical references and index.
  ISBN-13: 978-0-7377-3646-5 (hardcover)
  1. Music trade--Juvenile literature. 2. Music--Computer network resources--Juvenile literature. 3. Piracy (Copyright)--Juvenile literature. I. Aksomitis, Linda.
  ML3790.D67 2008
  384.3--dc22
                                     2007030381

CONTENTS

Music is a language understood around the world. The Internet magazine, Rootsworld, says, "Our focus is the music of the world: Africa, Asia, Europe, Pacifica and the Americas, the roots of the global musical milieu that has come to be known as world music, be it traditional folk music, jazz, rock or some hybrid. How is that defined? I don't know and don't particularly care at this point: it's music from someplace you aren't, music with roots, music of the world and for the world."

The term "World Music" was born in 1982 when World Music Day (Fête de la Musique) was initiated in France. Celebrated on the summer solstice, or June 21, every year, new artists perform freely in the street and concerts are held to celebrate virtually every type of music.

So why was World Music important enough for various countries (Belgium, Britain, Luxembourg, Germany, Switzerland, China, India, Lebanon, Malaysia, Morocco, Pakistan and others) to recognize it with a special day? Music is a form of cultural expression countries believe needs to be valued. It is a medium that can give a voice to those who may otherwise be disenfranchised, whether they're the street kids of America or the Quechua women of Peru. With the combination of lyrics, rhythm, and beat, performers tell stories and record histories. While listeners may not always understand the language, the other elements of music still convey a message.

Now, several decades after World Music Day began, the Internet allows users to celebrate World Music each and every day of the year with unlimited access to music from around the globe—by both established bands and emerging artists. A computer may hold French Manouche or Gypsy style music, tunes from Curaçao in the Dutch Antilles, and punk music by the band who practice in a garage down the street.

The Internet has provided musicians like rap artist Ludacris with less expensive ways of reaching larger audiences, but it also makes it easier for fans to acquire music without paying for it.

At the 48th Annual Grammy awards in February 2006, heavy metal artist, Slipknot, said of digital music and the Internet, "A kid that lives in a small town doesn't have access to a big chain store, and he deserves to see the show and hear the music just as much as a kid in New York City or L.A." Indeed, streaming video on the Internet provides access to concerts from anywhere in the world, as artists upload their soundtracks and video files to either their own web sites or communities such as MySpace, Second Life, ChristianRock.net, Reggae.com, and others.

Connecting artists with listeners creates a win-win situation on the Internet. The old way of promoting musicians required a big budget, and lots of time, to travel across the country on tour. Then, it was still a matter of luck whether or not individuals would see every group whose music they might enjoy. Schedules and venue limitations made it impossible to reach many would-be fans.

Just as it is more expensive to promote artists in the bricks-and-mortar world, it is also more expensive to produce albums for sale as DVDs. Digital-only releases are becoming more popular, nearly doubling in 2006 in the United States. In the United Kingdom during the same time, 30% of the industry released 37,000 albums were digital only. Reduced costs mean more albums, which in turn gives fans greater selection, and more musicians a start in the industry.

Today bands can build a following of fans before they ever sign with a record label or organize a tour. Bands like the indie/hip-hop fusion group, Gym Class Heroes (perform *The Queen and I*), and artist, Cassie (sings *Me and U*), were discovered on MySpace before landing major record deals. Other groups, such as the rock band, Clap Your Hands Say Yeah, sold 25,000 copies of its first release mostly through the Internet, thereby establishing their popularity first in cyberspace.

Fans using Internet World Music communities have many advantages. Once, fans had to purchase posters and hang out around performances to talk to an artist. Now, many established and emerging artists have a virtual presence, so fans can see photos and videos, read blogs, and ask questions twenty-four hours a day. The community also enables fans to join forums, where they can spread the word about their favorite performers, and learn about new artists from others.

Since the Internet has virtually unlimited storage, sound tracks never have to disappear once they lose their initial popularity. Universal Music, for example, announced in February of 2006 that it was beginning a project to make 10,000 older, out-of-print European albums available for download. This is not only great news for fans, but also for artists, since their creations may generate revenue, or income, for decades rather than a few years.

Indeed, lost revenue is one of the problems faced by the music industry as the Internet continues to grow, and digital World Music becomes more popular. Around half a million users download music every minute of every day in North America—many of them from pirate sources that do not pay royalties to performers or recorders. The following viewpoints take a critical look at

Apple, Inc. plays a major role in the Internet music industry by providing fans with iPods that can hold thousands of songs and the iTunes store where consumers can legally download music.

downloading music, who it impacts and how. In addition, the volume contains several appendixes to help the reader understand and explore the topic, including a thorough bibliography and a list of organizations to contact for further information. The appendix entitled "What You Should Know About Downloading Music" offers crucial facts about downloading music and its impact on young people. The appendix "What You Should Do About Downloading Music" offers tips to young people who may confront the issues surrounding downloading music in their own lives. With all these features, *Issues That Concern You: Downloading Music* provides an excellent resource for everyone interested in this pressing issue.

ONE

Downloading Free Music Helps the Music Industry

Janis Ian

In the following viewpoint, Janis Ian argues that free Internet music downloads are good for the music industry and its artists. Her contention is that the music industry had the same negative response to technology such as home tape recorders, cassettes, minidisks, videos, and MTV—none of which destroyed the industry. Using her own experience, she outlines how free music downloads brought people to her personal web site, and as a result she either sold CDs to them or they attended live shows she performed. She maintains that artists have the ear of the masses and can better their own lives by taking control of the situation with music downloads. Janis Ian is a multiple Grammy-award-winning musician and song writer.

When researching an article, I normally send e-mails to friends and acquaintances, who answer my request with opinions and anecdotes. But when I said I was planning to argue that free Internet downloads are good for the music industry and its artists, I was swamped.

I received over 300 replies—and every single one from someone legitimately in the music business.

Even more interesting than the e-mails were the phone calls. I don't know anyone at the National Academy of Recording Arts &

Janis Ian, "Why Free Downloads Help, Not Hurt," CnetNews.com, July 12, 2002. Reproduced by permission.

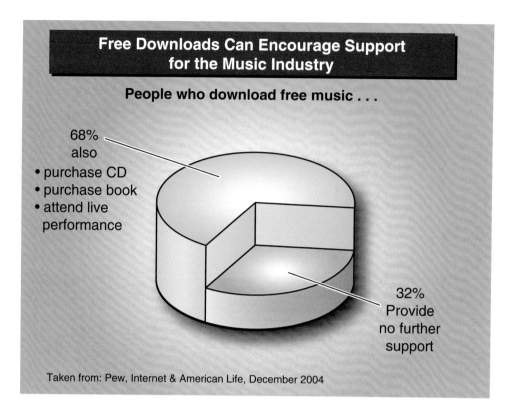

Free Downloads Can Encourage Support for the Music Industry

People who download free music . . .

68% also
• purchase CD
• purchase book
• attend live performance

32% Provide no further support

Taken from: Pew, Internet & American Life, December 2004

Sciences [NARAS] (home of the Grammy Awards), and I know Hilary Rosen (head of the Recording Industry Association of America, or RIAA) only in passing. Yet within 24 hours of sending my original e-mail, I'd received two messages from Rosen and four from NARAS, requesting that I call to "discuss the article." . . .

Industry Says Downloads Destroy Sales

Ms. Rosen, to be fair, stressed that she was only interested in presenting RIAA's side of the issue, and was kind enough to send me a fair amount of statistics and documentation, including a number of focus group studies RIAA had run on the matter.

However, the problem with focus groups is the same problem anthropologists have when studying peoples in the field: the moment the anthropologist's presence is known, everything changes. Hundreds of scientific studies have shown that any experimental group *wants to please the examiner.* For focus groups, this is particularly true. Coffee and donuts are the least of the payoffs.

The NARAS people were a bit more pushy. They told me downloads were "destroying sales," "ruining the music industry," and "costing *you* money."

Music Industry Has an Agenda

Costing *me* money? I don't pretend to be an expert on intellectual property law, but I do know one thing. If a music industry

Some listeners may use free downloads to learn more about an artist and then go out and purchase a CD.

executive claims I should agree with their agenda because it will make me more money, I put my hand on my wallet . . . and check it after they leave, just to make sure nothing's missing.

Am I suspicious of all this hysteria? You bet. Do I think the issue has been badly handled? Absolutely. Am I concerned about losing friends, opportunities, my 10th Grammy nomination, by publishing this article? Yeah. I am. But sometimes things are just wrong, and when they're that wrong, they have to be addressed.

The premise of all this ballyhoo is that the industry (and its artists) are being harmed by free downloading.

Nonsense.

Let's take it from my personal experience. My site gets an average of 75,000 hits a year. Not bad for someone whose last hit record was in 1975. When Napster was running full-tilt, we received about 100 hits a month from people who'd downloaded *Society's Child* or *At Seventeen* for free, then decided they wanted more information. Of those 100 people (and these are only the ones who let us know how they'd found the site), 15 bought CDs.

Not huge sales, right? No record company is interested in 180 extra sales a year. But that translates into $2,700, which is a lot of money in my book. And that doesn't include the people who bought the CDs in stores, or came to my shows.

Tape Recorders Didn't End the Music Industry

RIAA, NARAS and most of the entrenched music industry argue that free downloads hurt sales. More than hurt—it's destroying the industry.

Alas, the music industry needs no outside help to destroy itself. We're doing a very adequate job of that on our own, thank you.

The music industry had exactly the same response to the advent of reel-to-reel home tape recorders, cassettes, DATs, minidiscs, videos, MTV ("Why buy the record when you can tape it?") and a host of other technological advances designed to make the consumer's life easier and better. I know because I was there.

The only reason they didn't react that way publicly to the advent of CDs was because they believed CDs were uncopyable.

I was told this personally by a former head of Sony marketing, when they asked me to license *Between the Lines* in CD format at a reduced royalty rate. ("Because it's a brand new technology.")

Realistically, why do most people download music? To hear new music, and to find old, out-of-print music—not to avoid paying $5 at the local used CD store, or taping it off the radio, but to hear music they can't find anywhere else. Face it: Most people can't afford to spend $15.99 to experiment. And an awful lot of records are out of print; I have a few myself!

Free Downloads Provide Exposure

Everyone is forgetting the main way an artist becomes successful—exposure. Without exposure, no one comes to shows, no one buys CDs, no one enables you to earn a living doing what you love.

Again, from personal experience: In 37 years as a recording artist, I've created 25-plus albums for major labels, and I've *never* received a royalty statement that didn't show I owed *them* money. Label accounting practices are right up there with Enron. I make the bulk of my living from live touring, doing my own show. Live shows are pushed by my Web site, which is pushed by the live shows, and both are pushed by the availability of my music, for free, online. Who gets hurt by free downloads? Save a handful of super-successes like Celine Dion, none of us. We only get helped.

Most consumers have no problem paying for entertainment. If the music industry had a shred of sense, they'd have addressed this problem seven years ago, when people like Michael Camp were trying to obtain legitimate licenses for music online. Instead, the industrywide attitude was, "It'll go away". That's the same attitude CBS Records had about rock 'n' roll when Mitch Miller was head of A&R. (And you wondered why they passed on The Beatles and The Rolling Stones.)

NARAS and RIAA are moaning about the little mom-and-pop stores being shoved out of business; no one worked harder to shove them out than our own industry, which greeted every new mega-music store with glee, and offered steep discounts to Target,

WalMart, et al, for stocking their CDs. The Internet has zero to do with store closings and lowered sales.

And for those of us with major label contracts who want some of our music available for free downloading . . . well, the record companies own our masters, our outtakes, even our demos, and they won't allow it. Furthermore, they own our voices for the duration of the contract, so we can't post a live track for downloading even if we want to.

Zero Evidence That Free Online Music Financially Harms Anyone

If you think about it, the music industry should be rejoicing at this new technological advance. Here's a foolproof way to deliver music to millions who might otherwise never purchase a CD in a store. The cross-marketing opportunities are unbelievable. Costs are minimal, shipping nonexistent—a staggering vehicle for higher earnings and lower costs. Instead, they're running around like chickens with their heads cut off, bleeding on everyone and making no sense.

There is *zero* evidence that material available for free online downloading is financially harming anyone. In fact, most of the hard evidence is to the contrary.

The RIAA is correct in one thing—these are times of great change in our industry. But at a time when there are arguably only four record labels left in America (Sony, AOL Time Warner, Universal, BMG—and where is the RICO act when we need it?), when entire genres are glorifying the gangster mentality and losing their biggest voices to violence, when executives change positions as often as Zsa Zsa Gabor changed clothes, and "A&R" has become a euphemism for "Absent & Redundant," we have other things to worry about.

We'll turn into Microsoft if we're not careful, folks, insisting that any household wanting an extra copy for the car, the kids, or the portable CD player, has to go out and "license" multiple copies.

As artists, we have the ear of the masses. We have the trust of the masses. By speaking out in our concerts and in the press, we can do a great deal to dampen this hysteria, and put the blame for the sad state of our industry right back where it belongs—in the laps of record companies, radio programmers, and our own apparent inability to organize ourselves in order to better our own lives—and those of our fans.

If we don't take the reins, no one will.

Downloading Free Music Hurts the Music Industry

The Canadian Recording Industry Association

In the following viewpoint. The Canadian Recording Industry Association (CRIA) argues that downloading free music adversely affects both artists and the industry. They believe that if consumers want their favorite artists to succeed they need to support them, and the industry, by buying their music. In this viewpoint CRIA present a variety of myths believed by music consumers, and provide information to debunk each of the myths using industry information available to them. The Canadian Recording Industry Association is a non-profit trade organization that was founded in 1964 to represent the interests of Canadian companies that create, manufacture and market sound recordings.

Downloading Free Music Hurts the Music Industry

There is no doubt that the 'free music' mentality is adversely affecting artists and industry alike by devaluing an important component of culture and commerce. The fact is that the music business needs constant investment in order to bring new artists to the public and develop artist careers over the long term. There is also no doubt that downloading and CD-R burning are cutting into sales—the major means by which the majority of artists make a living from music. Live touring has always been a source of income, but it cannot fund an entire career, the expenses of going on the road mean that profits, while healthy in some cases, are in the majority of cases offset by the costs. Even when a new artist is discovered over the internet, unless enough people buy their records, either via a legitimate site or in a physical format, they won't be able to make a living.

Some artists of course do become big stars and with it they gain high financial rewards, but for the industry that has invested in them, those profits are ploughed back into funding new artists.

Consumers have to know that if they want a wide choice and variety of music, that if they want their favourite artists to succeed, they must support them by buying their music. . . .

Myth: Music Downloaded from the Internet Is Free

It is a common misconception that accessing so-called 'free music'—by downloading or burning music from the internet without the creator's permission and without paying for it—doesn't really hurt anyone.

Nothing could be further from the truth. Unauthorized uploading or copying is not free at all—it is the musicians and the people who invest in the music who are paying the price. The artists, first and foremost, the labels that have invested in them, the publishers who manage the copyright of their songs and the thousands of people involved in the many different areas of the music industry are all affected. Downloading and burning without permission doesn't fairly reward the efforts of those who create, develop and record music, and who depend on it for their livelihood.

More illegal copying and internet distribution means less sales, and that means less money for companies to invest in artists and music. This affects a whole community of people: the employee at the retail store that faces closure; the aspiring artist who won't get a deal because record companies have less money to invest in new talent; the entrepreneur who's making records with local kids; the act who is trying to survive from selling CDs on the road; and the artist whose first album just failed to sell enough to turn a profit. On top of that, there are the thousands of other people who depend upon music for their income: from the sound engineers and CD factory workers to the band managers and graphic artists. There are also countless music magazines, entrepreneurs trying to set up legitimate online sites, designers, specialist PR people. . . the list goes on.

Furthermore—copying music without permission is illegal. And just because it doesn't involve organized crime or knock-offs sold on street corners doesn't mean that it isn't taken very seriously.

Myth: Artists Are Immensely Rich
The overwhelming majority of artists are NOT rich. And it's not just a few tracks but virtually everything ever recorded. But the biggest losers are the upcoming artists because not paying for music means much less money to invest in them.

Which means it's the music lover who gets short-changed. Fewer artists get the chance to make their mark, and the labels are less likely to take a risk with more experimental music or niche genres. Consumers of 'free music' may get a short-term benefit, but at the long-term cost of hurting the artists they most admire, and new talent.

People who accuse the music industry of not producing any-thing new should give some thought to how that impacts on new artists. Think of the bands—and there are many who didn't make it big with their first or second album. Artists and bands need time to flourish, and if their early sales are cannibalized on the internet, they may never get the chance to record the second album.

Myth: The Music Industry Exaggerates the Effects of Free Downloads
There is overwhelming evidence that unauthorized copying and distribution means less music is sold.

For example, look at the way sales of albums have fallen while internet uploads have soared. During one four-month period of 2002, the number of music files available on pirate sites nearly doubled from 500 million to 900 million. At the same time global music sales in 2002 fell by around 7%. As a result around 250 million fewer albums were sold in 2002 than in 2001.

Uploading and mass copying weren't necessarily the only reason for this decline—but they definitely had a major impact.

In particular, sales of the top-selling artists are declining: in 2001 for the first time in many years no album sold more than ten million copies in the world's largest market, America—a pattern almost repeated in 2002 when only one album—Eminem's *The Eminem Show*—passed the ten million sales mark. And as sales of the bigger names fall, there are repercussions for the growth and support of new talent.

Perhaps the most worrying development is that the majority of people downloading music from the internet are young music fans, who are also the biggest consumers of music. 41% of young people in Europe who get music 'for free' say they buy less CDs, compared to only 19% who buy more.

Airtist, a French company, discourages music piracy by paying artists for works that are downloaded.

A whole new generation of music lovers is damaging the very diversity they look out for in music.

Myth: Free Downloads Promote Artists' Music and Boost Sales

We support the use of promotional material made available for free download—but only where the artists and other rights holders have authorized it for this purpose. This must be a choice that they make, not one forced upon them by others.

Making music available on the internet is a really exciting development for artists. The net can be a great tool for new acts who wish to drum up interest in their work.

It isn't true that making music 'free' will always promote the sales of that track or album, however. In fact research shows that downloading and burning is substituting sales significantly more than they are promoting them. Research in markets around the world shows that one third of active file-sharers spend less on music since they started getting it for free.

Most artists are happy for consumers to download their music—when it's legitimate and with their consent. And those who want to disseminate their music for free have the choice to do so.

[One Web site], for example, contains thousands of songs by aspiring artists—although it is a question how many artists, if any, have been able to embark on a career just using the internet. The fact is that most people who go online to download are much more likely to go for known artists—even if new to them—rather than complete unknowns.

It is those who think that they have the right to 'share' music illegally with millions of individuals without having paid for it that are damaging the music industry, and as a consequence are threatening the careers of budding artists before they even begin.

Myth: The Music Industry Wants to Stop the Advance of Technology

Technology is not the enemy of music—quite the opposite. There has always been a healthy relationship between advances in technology and the music business: from the Edison cylinder, through vinyl, tape, and the CD, to the MP3 file. The impact of digital technology has opened doors for artists and many others involved in music; allowing more experimentation and sophisticated home recording, online real time musical collaborations, webcasts, enhanced sound— and the ability to share all that with a wider global audience.

The music industry will always make use of new technology— for example Super Audio CDs and DVD Audio, as well as the opportunities that new 3G phones bring. Technology is also helping the industry to transfer thousands of tracks in artists' back catalogues into digital format.

But while the methods of recording or distribution might change, what doesn't is that artists and those who work with them depend upon copyright and getting paid for their livelihood.

Myth: There Are No Legitimate Services so Users Fall Back on Illegitimate Ones

A number of legal online services are expected to launch in Canada this fall. Puretracks, a Canadian service, has already announced a fall launch date.

These sites offer better quality of product and service than illegal alternatives. Many are now offering transfer to portable devices. Potentially, hundreds of thousands of songs will be legally made available at cost-effective prices.

And it's just not good enough to say if I can't get it legally, I'll steal it.

Myth: Piracy on the Internet May Be a Problem, but Nothing Can Stop It

It is a huge problem, but it has to be stopped and it can be. The recording industry has many ways of stopping illegal downloading and file-sharing; from education programs and the launch of legal alternatives to technological 'blocks' and—where necessary—deterrence through legal action.

The music industry has launched many initiatives to educate consumers and businesses around the world about the consequences of illegal online activity. Many people who enjoy music are simply unaware of the effect their actions have on bands and artists.

Everyone knows that one of the best ways to stop people from using the illegal sites is to provide them with good alternatives. Many companies are investing huge amounts in developing legal alternatives. It takes time because it's hard to compete with free, but it is happening.

We're also seeing the start of new systems used for a better electronic delivery of music on the internet. Digital rights management tools are being used to help track music online, so that everyone who needs to be is paid—all the way down the line. New technology is also being used in ever more sophisticated anti-copy control devices for music, similar to those already used on DVDs and computer software.

But there's more to stopping mass copyright theft than by just investing in new legitimate services. Indeed, those new services are not going to flourish if there isn't a fair space for them to develop without being stifled by online piracy. So those who ignore copyright laws should not expect an easy ride.

Copyright exists to protect the rights of artists, allowing them to determine whether and how copying, distributing, broadcasting and other uses of their works take place. In addition, legislation around the world is being adopted to improve rights and technological protection to help fight piracy in the online world. People who breach copyright have to be prepared to face the appropriate legal penalties, including fines.

Myth: File Sharing and Burning Is Just Like Home Taping
File sharing via the internet cannot be likened to copying tapes deck to deck at home. That's like comparing someone physically copying a letter to a printing house churning out hundreds of copies a minute of the same letter—and then making it available to absolutely everyone around the world for free.

CD recordable (CD-R) copying is comparable to a home version of the high-speed mass production of CDs in factories. You could burn as many as 200 albums onto multiple CD-R discs in less time than it takes you to read this web page. It's cheaper too—20 years ago the first CD manufacturing facility cost US$1billion. Now the same capability is available to home users for less than $150.

The damage this sort of copying causes to music is enormous. But it also presents other dangers to the unwitting consumer. If you use a peer-to-peer service, you open your computer and all the information you've stored in it up to hundreds of strangers—simply at the touch of a button. When you use a file-sharing service you may unwittingly be acting as a 'mass distributor'; as whenever you're online every other user around the world has the ability to access your hard drive. And this could lead to problems with your personal computer, including the transmission of viruses.

Myth: Recording Companies Don't Get Artists' Tracks Online Quickly Enough

While it is very easy for anyone to upload an MP3 music file onto the net and give it away for nothing, what takes time is to do so in such a way that the online product is tracked through the process, with the artists, publishers, record companies, third party retailers all being paid their share of the price. The systems for doing this have had to be created from scratch and there have been complex negotiations between all the relevant parties in order to get the music licensed for digital sale.

Second, it is not true to say that record companies have not got their music online quickly enough. The music industry is far more advanced than any other in terms of producing its product for digital sale. What is true is that the appearance of the MP3 file format has meant that the music industry has been forced to grapple with issues of theft of intellectual property on the internet far sooner than other industries. Unlike most products where the internet is simply used to help sell the physical product, with music the virtual online copy is practically the same as the physical product.

The speed with which the MP3 music file spread over the internet meant that as the music companies started to digitize their product, set up payment systems and invest in companies, they were already in a situation where they were competing with free. And trying to compete against an over 99% pirate market on the internet is very difficult. Isn't it ridiculous to expect a record company who has to invest a huge amount in its artists to compete with a distributor who is giving music away?

Myth: There's Only One Answer to Piracy—Lower CD Prices

In an ideal world everything would be free. Artists wouldn't need money to buy instruments. Record companies wouldn't invest money in recording. Designers and retailers would donate their time and talent scouts would not have any costs. Best of all, tax wouldn't exist. But let's face it, this is the real world. And legitimate companies who invest in and create music cannot be expected to compete with music taken and given away 'for free'. Whether we like it or not, all businesses have overheads and the business of music is no exception. Huge costs are spent on developing talent, from finding it to recording, producing, promoting, marketing and distributing it.

It is also true that most criticism of CD prices springs from a misunderstanding of how much royalty, distribution, marketing and artist and repertoire development is reflected in the price of every CD that's sold. That's the real costs of a CD—not the cost of the disc itself.

It is another myth that studio executives pocket huge profits on everything they release. Profit in the business is rare—for every ten CDs the record companies put time and money into, generally only one brings a return on the original investment. Meanwhile the recording industry reinvests up to 25% of its turnover in new artists.

Music is still excellent value for money compared with other entertainment products; the 'cost per hour' of consuming music is significantly cheaper than books and other print media, cinema-going and mobile phone use. Buying an album is an investment in music that you will own for life.

THREE

Some Artists Support File-Sharing of Their Music

Holmes Wilson

In the following viewpoint, Holmes Wilson, of the Downhill Battle Web site, interviews music artist M.I.A. to show how one artist has taken advantage of free music downloads to launch her career. She views the big record companies as the villains in the controversy over file-sharing music, and sees the Internet as a great way to create songs that spread quickly around the world. M.I.A. (Maya Arulpragasam) signed with XL Recordings and used the Internet to distribute a mix tape of her first album. When the album, *Arular*, launched, it made her a mini-sensation. Downhill Battle is a non-profit organization working to support participatory culture and build a fairer music industry.

M.I.A.'s History

Holmes: So anyway, the thing I'm interested in is what you think about this whole music piracy thing, and how you think it relates to pop. That's the broad thing I'm interested in, because we do this website about how piracy is changing the way people participate in pop music.

   M.I.A.: I mean the thing is, it's really hard for someone like me because I made my music on something that cost like 300 pounds, my whole set up was just so homemade and it was in my bedroom and I demo'd all my tracks and I got signed straight out of the bedroom. And I used to hustle for studio time and get in like 5 hours every six weeks or something like that and so like it was always about empowering yourself and being able to survive with no money and being able to produce out of nothing and—you know—I still bum fares on the train and stuff, you know what I mean? I can't help it. . . .

And because I came through the channels that I came up through it wasn't dependent on the record company, and radio, and TV, and all that sorta stuff and magazine culture and whatever and I tried to come up and do it without any of their help, and they didn't give me any help.

Technology Gives Musicians Control

Holmes: Did you explicitly try to do that, or was that just how it happened? Were you like "I wanna do it without them" or did it just happen without them?

M.I.A.: I never fit in to that. I was always on the wrong side of the tracks and I was always feeling like I'd rather work out things that help people and empower people than to join the machine and perpetuate a certain idea that I don't believe in, so it was always about—for me it was always really about teaching people to just be honest and be straight, and be normal, and be grounded, and rely on your own things that you have and that you have around you. And in that sense, technology of course the obvious thing is that it does free up things and free up music for people.

Holmes: Because you can make it easier? Or because of the distribution? Or. . .

M.I.A.: Well, it's like . . . when you're an artist and you first start making work, the thing that you're led by is to make work and get it out to people, and that's just direct, you make it and then it's out and you have no care in the world and, f--- it, you've survived for $5 a day before and you can still carry on doing it. And in that sense I'm just like yeah, music is good for people so let 'em have it and in that way you don't have to censor it and if the idea is to make music more interesting for people than it's

GREAT that you don't have to go through these stupid machines because you can make music whatever you want it to be about and you can communicate and talk to people and no one's gonna censor you. . . .

Holmes: So I come from an activism background, like doing anti-sweatshop activism, protest, etc, and I kind of feel like, you know, the music industry, what does it have to do with the rest of corporate control in different parts of the political system? It sort of feels like if we get pop culture back . . . if we get that piece of pop culture back, we'd get a lot.

M.I.A.: Yeah, and the only way to do that is through the internet. . . .

Record Companies Are the Villains

Holmes: What do you think. . . and I guess you're approaching this more from the art angle than the political action angle. . . but if people out there want to do things to take music back from corporations, what do you think they should do?

M.I.A.: . . . I think the only way you can do it is to support songs that are not big on the radio, but to still give that artist alternative ways they can exist. Because that's really it, you know, the thing is, you can file share and you can bootleg and you can download, but then you have to make the artist survive, long enough that they can sustain themselves, so how do you make someone sustain themselves and. . . feed them, basically. I mean one of the things is artists are going to have to kind of be humble in what they want, and not start wearing the million pound f---ing diamond necklace around their neck because they don't need it, you know, and the people have to compromise and be like, o.k., you might not buy the album but you go and see a show, so you keep the . . . ability for the artist to go out.

Holmes: Do you see a lot of the people who like you doing that?

M.I.A.: Well I see. . . that's the thing I mean that's how the underground and the alternative scenes exist I guess. . . artists like. . . well there's tons of people, tons of musicians that exist probably on doing shows and selling their song to, you know, something. . . and then sustaining themselves. But I think, you know Peaches [Musician, Merrill Beth Nisker, whose work focuses on gender identity], it's one of those sort of things where I don't know how much she gets fileshared, you know what I mean?

Holmes: Probably a lot. Or probably like. . . a moderate amount.

M.I.A.: Yeah. I think both sides, everybody has to be fair in this you know, and we all know the record companies, well I guess they are like the villains in all this.

Holmes: Should we boycott them?

M.I.A.: Ah, I think that's impossible really. Not until you've made a better way, until the people have figured out a better way to distribute outside the internet and stuff. To me, that's why it's really important that I start hanging onto the fact that I was coming from a global position and that I don't have a localized area

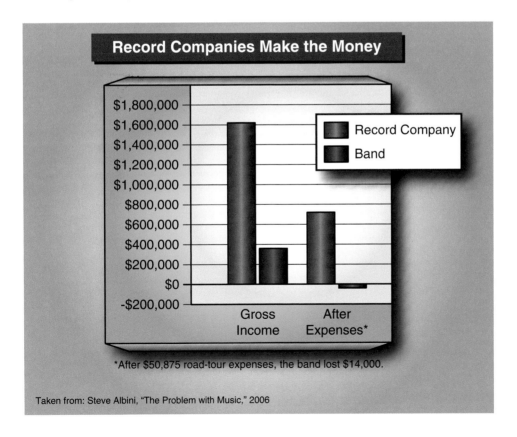

Record Companies Make the Money

*After $50,875 road-tour expenses, the band lost $14,000.

Taken from: Steve Albini, "The Problem with Music," 2006

or anything like that, because it is so much about the internet, because of that. I know that kids in Sri Lanka can hear my music through the internet and when I get to Sri Lanka they don't even have anything in the villages and its been war torn for twenty years, but you always find a little internet shack, you know? So I know that there's interest in the third world and places to have that information at your finger tips at the same time as everybody else in the west, whereas, they don't have record shops and they have to go buy a cd player for like a month's wages. So in that sense its really important for us to just say, well, it's one big planet,

Los Angeles musician Kevin Martin is using file-sharing to promote his new band instead of relying on traditional methods which can be more expensive.

and if a song comes out then its just about spreading it and not really about localized record companies. I mean the reason why right now you're dependant on Sony or Universal or whatever is that right now they've got distribution all over the world that can get your music out. So that artists, to some extent, especially me. . . I mean I had no musical background, history, or idea about how it worked, and I was always like you know, I'm gonna watch my back. . . . And I'm the most, like, mean, hard, cautious, cynical person you can think of when it comes to the authority figure, you know? but at some point I had to go, yeah—you know I signed to an indie in London, and then how far can they get it across? And then I signed to interscope and I know they can get more records out to more people, so then they have a choice. They can go buy a Brittney [Spears] record or they can buy your record. So. . . the one thing you have to fight with all these corporations. . . television, radio, even the government. . . everybody has got people down for the mental age of about twelve, and that's why they feed us shit, because they think that we're really really dumb, and that's why the internet is so refreshing, because you can address people on their level. You can just go, yeah you're smart, this is what's going on, and you can just start the conversation on a certain level. But the rest of the world is just set to a lowest common denominator, and they think that you're really thick. And I was so bored of that, you know? Especially when you live in England, and you stand up and you try to get anything made or do work or approach any corporations, and they always assume that the people out there are so dumb, therefore you have to water everything down, you have to dilute it, censor it. . . .

Promoting Independent Artists Works on the Internet

Holmes: Well the problem is that all the smart people out there still like the stupid stuff [meaningless lyrics].

    M.I.A.: That little pop. . . twinkle thing.

    Holmes: . . . and because we all want to dance to music that everybody else knows, because it's more fun that way.

M.I.A.: But then it comes back to (the question of) how you get that stuff out, without selling yourself to a record label. And it's like the internet is the only thing. But then, it means your skin, and you can't get out onto the road, can't do shows, and you're still working at the shop. But you've made a song and it's out and it could be all over the world. So maybe we're just in the early days and there's another way of doing it, and i-tunes kind of makes sense I suppose because it's like 79p a song, but then that still goes through the managers.

Paying for File-Shared Music Would Work

Holmes: Well if you're on a major it still goes through the managers, but if you're not then it's a pretty good deal. There's this one system that people have been kicking around where they say o.k. well, there's file sharing software out there, let's legalize it and then track it, so every time someone downloads something it's tracked, and then charge people. You know how they're suing people in America? Well what if you said o.k. you pay five dollars a month and you don't get sued. You get internet at thirty five dollars a month, and pay five dollars a month for music. That five dollars goes into a pool and gets distributed according to how many downloads you get. Would you go for that, if you were a politician?

M.I.A.: Yeah definitely.

Holmes: It's one of those things that they don't want to do because it means less control. Because anybody can come up and make money, and get popular.

M.I.A.: It would make it so fierce though. It would make the industry so fierce.

Holmes: Yeah because if you can get it out there then it sells. And the other thing is, if an album gets leaked, say an album gets leaked six weeks before it comes out, then it doesn't matter. People still get paid.

M.I.A.: Yeah I suppose it's kind of like, early days, but I'll vote for it. I mean I've done it in such a higgledy-piggledy sort of way, you know my album was out, and then I did a mix-tape, everybody downloaded the album, everybody downloaded the mix tape, and then "Galang" came out and it was more widespread on the internet. It never got radio play, you know what I mean?

Holmes: The video is amazing.

M.I.A.: Yeah and I get like two million hits a month on my website or whatever and it's kind of like, you know, I totally believe in the power of the internet. (laughing) I BELIEVE!

FOUR

Some Artists Don't Support File-Sharing of Their Music

MusicUnited.org

> In the following viewpoint. MusicUnited.org quotes numerous artists and songwriters who feel peer to peer (P2P) unauthorized downloading of their music has negatively impacted on their income. Musicians compare illegal downloads to such things as: stealing CDs from a store: breaking into someone's home and taking everything they've accumulated over a lifetime: and taking artists' right to privacy, by removing their ability to decide which of their songs or recordings becomes available to the public. MusicUnited is the collective expression of a broad movement of people and institutions involved in the recording industry—including songwriters, recording artists, record companies, musicians and the Recording Industry Association of America.

Artists and songwriters of every style and genre are speaking out against illegal copying. . . . Here's what some of them have to say. . . .

Phil Galdston, Grammy Award-Winning Composer, Lyricist Music Publisher: "Our livelihood is seriously and negatively impacted by unauthorized downloading of our work through peer-to-peer networks. . . . Every time someone downloads a song of mine without

MusicUnited.org, "What the Artists and Songwriters Have to Say," 2005. Reproduced by permission.

my permission, I am losing all that follows from it: the ability to support my family, the capital needed to continue to re-invest in my business, and the economic incentive to continue to create."

Amber, Top Five Billboard Chart Hit "This is Your Night": "Music is a very important element in our society, since mankind existed—it lifts spirits, it inspires and helps people to get through difficult situations. We, as musicians and songwriters, are the neutral politicians of this world—music is a global language—understood everywhere—it raises tremendous amounts of money for many beneficial institutions—whatever downloading does to us and our families, you also deprive many people in need out there, that benefit from our help and our music."

Rivers Rutherford, Co-writer of 2001 billboard's Country Song of the Year: "The average songwriter has to be very fortunate to make any money at all from his craft. Illegal internet downloading significantly reduces the income of people who are not making millions from touring, T-shirt sales, etc., but merely trying to make a decent living. Downloading can literally make it impossible for a songwriter to support himself with his craft."

Dixie Chicks, Grammy Award Winning and Two-Time Diamond Award Recipient: "It may seem innocent enough, but every time you illegally download music a songwriter doesn't get paid. And, every time you swap that music with your friends a new artist doesn't get a chance. Respect the artists you love by not stealing their music. You're in control. Support music, don't steal it."

Nelly, Multi-Platinum Hip-Hop Artist, Number One Hit "Hot In Herre": "As an artist you hate for someone to break into your home and take everything that you've accumulated over the last how many ever years you've been in this game. It's like a dream to get here, and then once you get here to have someone take it from under you is real tough to deal with. We really look at it as stealing, because, that's just it, to us it's black and white, either you pay for it or you don't. And, you're not paying for it."

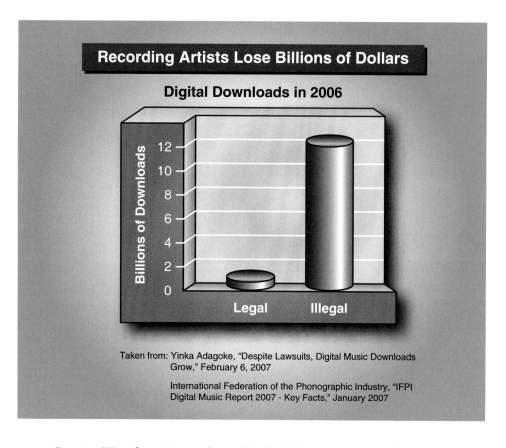

Recording Artists Lose Billions of Dollars

Digital Downloads in 2006

Billions of Downloads

12
10
8
6
4
2
0

Legal   Illegal

Taken from: Yinka Adagoke, "Despite Lawsuits, Digital Music Downloads Grow," February 6, 2007

International Federation of the Phonographic Industry, "IFPI Digital Music Report 2007 - Key Facts," January 2007

Stevie Wonder, Legendary Multi-Platinum Award-Winning Artist: "Record companies, publishers, radio stations, retailers, artists and others in our industry must take a very strong position against the stealing of our writing and music or else those writings and music will become as cheap as the garbage in the streets."

Missy Elliot, Writer, Producer, Rapper, Singer: "Hip Hop has always been about the attainable dream—about running your own business, your own club, your own fanzine. Turning your back on bootleggers helps us pave the way for the next generation of entrepreneurs. We do our best to bring you the latest, hottest beats, and we appreciate it when our fans show their love and respect by going in that record store and buying the finished product."

Musiq, Singer, Platinum Award Winning Urban Music Artist, "AIJUSWANASEING": "I think that people do need to be educated on the seriousness of music piracy because it cuts into hard working people's money, especially the artists—people like me. So, it catches my attention. I don't think that it's cool, because if I'm putting in all of this work to see all of these returns and I don't see the full capacity of my returns, because somebody is cutting in on it, we've got to do something about it. Right now you've got people thinking, 'What . . . I'm only just doing this, I'm only just doing that.' But, you're only just doing this and this person is only just doing that, and it's chipping away and it's chipping away and chipping away. And, you don't see it, but it's a serious thing."

Britney Spears, Multi-Platinum Award Winning Artist "Oops! . . . I Did It Again": "Would you go into a CD store and steal a CD? It's the same thing, people going into the computers and logging on and stealing our music. It's the exact same thing, so why do it?"

Sean (P. Diddy) Combs, Multi-Platinum Award Winning Artist, Producer, Founder and CEO of Bad Boy Entertainment: "As an artist who has dedicated his life to music and the music business, I have seen what illegal music copying has done and continues to do to new and established musicians. I understand why people download music, but for me and my fellow artists, this is our livelihood. When you make an illegal copy, you're stealing from the artist. It's that simple. Every single day we're out here pouring our hearts and souls into making music for everyone to enjoy. What if you didn't get paid for your job? Put yourself in our shoes!"

Vanessa Carlton, Singer/Songwriter, "A Thousand Miles" and Gold-Award Winning Artist for "Be Not Nobody": "I think it's great that there are even more avenues today to expose music and new artists. And I'm all for getting a taste of something before you buy it, but when it becomes more than a taste and people begin hoarding the entire work, it becomes piracy which results in a system in which artists are not being rewarded for their works. Works which they put everything they have into creating and then working their asses off to support and promote."

Glen Ballard, Award-Winning Songwriter/Producer; including Alanis Morrisette's "Jagged Little Pill," Dave Matthews Band's "Everyday": "Piracy is an insidious act performed in an almost offhanded way by people who would never consider stealing anything else. Few people involved in the act of downloading music illegally would walk into a retail store and steal a CD of the same music, or take a CD player or computer to reproduce the music. It's highly likely that you would be caught and arrested, and it's also obvious that taking something without paying for it is a fundamentally unfair act. But as everyone knows, you can steal from the Internet without the fear of being caught. But the fundamental unfairness remains. We should honor our artists and their art by paying for their work, like you would pay for anything else. I work with artists, writers, singers and musicians who strive every day to be better at communicating. It's hard work, and requires years of dedication. They deserve to be compensated for the joy they bring to so many others."

Renée Fleming, Grammy-Award Winning Classical Artist, "Bel Canto": "A new recording is an immensely personal and heart-felt statement, representing the culmination of countless hours of work and involving the collaboration and commitment of numerous dedicated artists. In the case of my recordings, this can sometimes include an orchestra and chorus—literally hundreds of musicians—not to mention producers, technicians and many others who depend on this income. We are thrilled that people want to hear what we have done. They can show their respect and support by purchasing the CD legally. If not, we will all soon be unable to continue to make quality recordings."

Brian Wilson, Rock and Roll Hall of Fame Inductee and Founding Member of the Beach Boys: "There are two issues here. First is the creative issue. When I decide not to release a piece of MY WORK, there is always a good reason for it. I created it, I should have the final say on whether it should be released or not. The other, of course, is obvious. It's the financial issue. I would never expect to hire anyone and not pay them for their services. When people

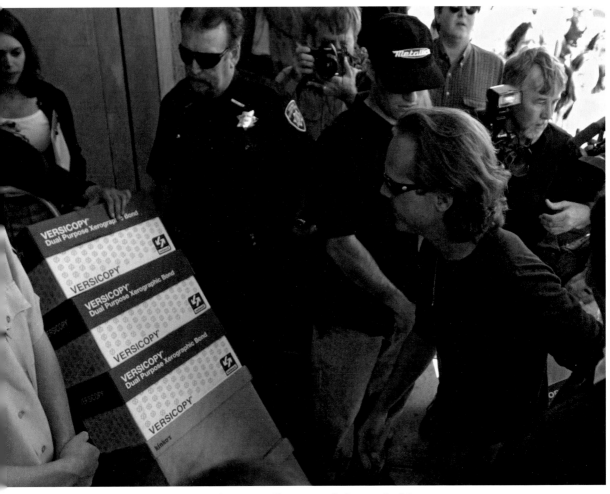

Lars Ulrich, drummer for Metallica, with boxes holding a report of names of more than 317,000 people they claimed were illegally downloading Metallica's music from Napster.

buy counterfeits, the artist and the creator are not getting paid for their work. It's as simple as that. If my fans feel that I am unable to decide what work of mine should be released and feel that I do not have the right to make a living doing it, then why bother? The bottom line is the fan who is saying, "Oh man you're the greatest," is in reality stealing from you and your family, and more importantly not respecting your judgment on what you think is appropriate to bear your name."

Carl Sturken & Evan Rogers, Grammy-Award Winning Songwriters/ Producers: "How would you feel if someone came in to your home and began taking everything they wanted that looked cool, and gave you nothing in return. Pretty crazy, right? That's how we feel about the piracy of music. When we were growing up, saving your money to go to the record store was one of the more important things in life. Most of the teenagers we know today are far more interested in buying a CD burner and downloading whatever music they want for free. We think that pretty much says it all."

Elton John, Legendary Grammy Award Winning Artist: "I am excited about the opportunities presented by the Internet because it allows artists to communicate directly with fans. But the bottom line must always be respect and compensation for creative work. I am against Internet piracy and it is wrong for to promote stealing from artists online."

Shaggy, Grammy Award Winner, "Best Reggae Album— 'Boombastic'": "I understand how it will help life for unsigned bands. It is definitely a window to showcase a lot of bands that probably wouldn't be getting to hear from a lot of these majors, but at the same time you all need to pay us now . . . I mean, straight up! This is some hard work. I was in the military for four years, man, and I'm telling you the music business is some hard work. . . . You need some sort of pension. And if they can't regulate it to where the artist gets paid, well, then it's not that great of an idea because even the unsigned artists, at some point, they're going to want to get paid for their things also."

Steven Curtis Chapman, Grammy-Award Winning Christian Artist: "A lot more goes into a CD than it may appear. The price of a CD doesn't just go back to the record company. Everyone who works with me to record and distribute my music makes a living and supports their families from CD sales as well. It's a big network of people from my co-producer, the engineers, my band all the way to assembly line people who help to manufacture the CDs and the truck drivers who get them to the stores. There are some new legitimate websites like burnitfirst.com that provide an alternative to illegal burning. I want to encourage my listeners to use sites such as this, and to buy instead of burning illegally. On behalf of the team who works alongside me, we'd appreciate it."

Trent Reznor, member of Nine Inch Nails: "Just because technology exists where you can duplicate something, that doesn't give you the right to do it. There's nothing wrong with giving some tracks away or bits of stuff that's fine. But it's not everybody's right. Once I record something, it's not public domain to give it away freely. And that's not trying to be the outdated musician who is trying to 'stop technology.' I love technology."

FIVE

The Music Industry Uses Various Methods to Stop Illegal Downloads

International Federation of the Phonographic Industry

International Federation of the Phonographic Industry (IFPI) states that there are various methods the industry uses to stop illegal downloading of music. Taking action against illegal services and peer to peer (P2P) networks give the legitimate market opportunities to grow. The IFPI provide education aimed at various demographic groups and users to enhance awareness of the issues. In addition, they note that P2P spyware, malicious code like viruses and Trojan horses, along with network worms, are playing a significant role in stopping the illegal sharing of files. IFPI is a worldwide organization, with its membership comprising some 1400 record companies in around 70 countries.

The emergence of legitimate digital music services is playing a key role in pushing back of online piracy. Today consumers are offered the vast catalogue of record companies' repertoire via diverse channels. In 2005 this amounted to a fast-growing US$1.1 billion market.

There are now more than 360 legal digital music services offering over three million songs to consumers in over 40 countries.

The Recording Industry Takes Legal Action

The recording industry has taken action against illegal services and P2P networks to give the legitimate market the space to grow. Actions have been brought against illegal file-sharers in 17 countries outside the US. The latest wave of nearly 2,000 cases was announced in April 2006.

These actions have been taken against large-volume uploaders who are distributing hundreds or thousands of copyrighted files on P2P networks. Profiles of these individuals vary markedly. They come from all walks of life ranging from a French chef to a Finnish carpenter. Settlements have averaged $12,633.

Independent research from market analysts Jupiter carried out in November 2005 suggests that legal action is having an impact. More than a third of Europeans who file-share said they have cut back or stopped their activities. This research also found that in the two biggest European markets, the UK and Germany, more people regularly buy music from legitimate services (5%) than regularly download music illegally (4%).

Internet Download Sales (millions of single tracks)

Country	Q1 2005	Q1 2006	Annual Growth
United States	76.2	144.0	89%
United Kingdom	4.5	11.5	152%
Japan	1.1	5.9	434%

Taken from: IFPI Piracy Report 2006

Research by TNS in the UK conducted in March 2006 suggests that more than half of people (56%) who have begun downloading in the last six months are using legal services, compared with just two-in-five people (41%) who have been downloading for more than a year.

Napster began using a subscription model after they were sued for copyright infringement over large numbers of illegal downloads from their service.

Education Promotes Legal Services

Education about copyright has a vital role to play in promoting a digital music business. IFPI runs multi-country educational projects aimed at enhancing awareness of copyright and issues surrounding music on the internet. These have been cited as best practice by the European Commission, endorsed by the International Chamber of Commerce and jointly launched with governments including Austria, Italy, Ireland, Hong Kong and Netherlands. They include:

Young People, Music and the Internet is a clear and simple guide aimed at parents. It explains "file-sharing" and "peer-to-peer" as well as how the technology works, helping them to keep their children safe, secure and legal on the internet. It has been translated into six languages and is available from www.pro-music.org and on the charity Childnet's website www.childnet-int.org/music. Most recently a Chinese language version of the guide has been launched in partnership with the Hong Kong government.

Digital File Check is freely-available software for all computer users to download from www.ifpi.org. It can help remove or block any of the unwanted file-sharing programmes commonly used to distribute copyrighted files illegally. It allows consumers to avoid becoming unwitting illegal file-sharers.

www.pro-music.org is a website branded "everything you need to know about music online" available in six languages, that acts as a gateway to more than 350 legitimate sites and is a central resource of information about music on the internet.

Instant messages have been sent to more than 53 million heavy illegal music uploaders in 17 countries, warning them to stop their activities.

Copyright Use and Security for Companies and Governments is a guide for employers, clarifying their responsibilities to keep their computer networks free from copyright infringement. The guide is produced jointly with the Motion Picture Association and International Video Federation and is endorsed by the International Chamber of Commerce. Copies can be obtained from IFPI.

National campaigns have been run by various IFPI national affiliates, such as the 'Truefan' kite mark for legal music websites in the Netherlands; a film aimed at young people called 'A thousand jobs in the music industry' in France and a lesson pack for schools produced in cooperation with the Ministry of Education in Finland.

Legal Action Works

The legal landscape for P2P networks changed significantly in 2005 and early 2006. A string of court judgements across the world established liability of P2P operators for the infringement that they promote and benefit—from rejecting the notion that unauthorized file-sharing is innocent, legal or victimless. There were also key judgements against other unlicensed services:

- In June 2005 the US Supreme Court ruled (in *MGM v Grokster*) that file-sharing services that distribute software with the object of promoting its use to infringe copyright can be held liable for the resulting infringements.
- In August 2005 Seoul District Court ordered Soribada, a Korean P2P service, to prevent its users [from swapping] copyrighted songs, or shut down.
- In September 2005 the Federal Court of Australia held that Kazaa was guilty of copyright infringement and ordered it to shut down or implement copyright filters.
- Also in September 2005, a Taiwanese court issued a criminal conviction to the directors of the Kuro P2P service which was in breach of intellectual property rules.
- November 2005 saw the Grokster P2P network agree to shut down operations in light of the US Supreme Court's ruling.
- In February 2006 the Danish Supreme Court ruled that under EU law, ISPs can be obliged to terminate the connections of customers who illegally upload material.
- May 2006 saw the American operators of BearShare agree to cease to operate any music or film download services and sell its assets to the legal file-sharing service iMesh.

- In June 2006 the Dutch Court of Appeals ruled against zoek mp3.com, effectively declaring that deep linking to infringing mp3 files is illegal in the Netherlands.

Viruses Help Stop Illegal File-Sharing

Concern about P2P spyware, viruses and threats to privacy have played as significant a part in deterring illegal file-sharing as well as legal actions by the music industry.

StopBadware.org, an organisation based in Harvard and Oxford Universities, says that 60 million people's computers in the US now have software that hampers the machine's performance. The group named Kazaa, one of the most popular P2P networks, as a prime source of such spyware.

Research from TruSecure concluded that 45 per cent of the executable files downloaded through Kazaa contain malicious code like viruses and Trojan horses after testing 4,500 such files.

P2P network worms also spread using these services. The most widespread are Kazaa P2P network worms which usually locate a Kazaa client shared folder and copy themselves there with an attractive name, of a popular song for example. Sometimes such worms replace real sound files and can host dangerous viruses.

Many users find themselves downloading the wrong files as the names and descriptions for them can be misleading and users can end up with inappropriate material. In some cases paedophiles have used P2P communities to distribute pornographic materials and make contact with children.

Research by analysts Jupiter showed that of those Europeans who said they have given up or cut down their illegal file-sharing activity, 35 per cent did so because they were worried about the effects of viruses on their computers.

The Spread of Pre-Release Piracy

New releases are the lifeblood of the music industry and pre-release piracy has a serious effect on legal sales and on record companies' ability to reinvest in new artists.

Pre-release piracy is a growing problem for the music industry. New recordings can be posted on the internet through a range of distribution platforms including websites and peer-to-peer (P2P) networks. They have the potential to reach mass distribution within hours. Already in 2006, key new releases by Placebo, Franz Ferdinand, The Strokes, The Flaming Lips and, most recently, The Red Hot Chili Peppers, were available illegally online weeks before release.

The Family Entertainment and Copyright Act (2005) in the US singled out pre-release piracy as a problem and allowed for penalties to be imposed on those who pirate copyrighted works before they are released into the legitimate market.

The new generation of web-based pirate distribution—web and FTP sites—are frequently the first source of illegal music on the internet. News of the leak quickly spreads over blogs and chat rooms and files begin to appear in P2P networks. This has a multiplying effect over the subsequent period of weeks.

IFPI and its member record companies actively combat pre-release piracy, concentrating as closely as possible on the source of the problem. The priority is to tackle the first leaks on the internet, thereby limiting the subsequent spread of illegal copies, and potentially stopping millions of illegal downloads.

SIX

Legal Action Doesn't Stop Illegal Downloads

Yinka Adegoke

In the following viewpoint Yinka Adegoke maintains that despite lawsuits, illegal digital music downloads continue to grow, producing loses of millions of dollars in annual sales each year for the music industry. She indicates that peer to peer (p2p) file sharing, which allows anonymous users to exchange digital music files freely, is to blame. Yinka Adegoke is a writer with Reuters in New York, as part of the technology, media and telecoms team. She left a career as Deputy Editor, *New Media Age,* in London, after six years of reporting on the digital media industry to join Reuters in 2005.

Despite success in suing people who download music illegally and in reaching deals with personal networking sites like YouTube, the music industry is still bleeding millions of dollars in sales to online piracy.

It is a major issue for an industry that is desperately trying to boost revenue from legal downloads to make up for falling sales of Compact Discs, which declined 23 percent globally between 2000 to 2006.

How Big Is the Problem?

To get an idea of the size of the problem, Eric Garland of Web consultants Big Champagne estimates that more than 1 billion digital tracks are illegally traded for free each month.

By comparison, Apple Inc.'s iTunes Music Store, which has more than 70 percent of legal digital music sales in the United States, has sold only a bit more than 2 billion songs since its launch in 2003.

The problem is so-called peer-to-peer (P2P) networks such as Gnutella and BitTorrent that link millions of personal computers and allow anonymous users to exchange digital music files for free over the Internet.

Lawsuits Only Help A Little

Since the music industry started winning lawsuits against individuals in the last few years, the growth in the number of people using illegal file-sharing software has slowed significantly, but nonetheless it is still growing.

In spite of several high-profile lawsuits, like the one against Napster, some people claim that the number of illegal downloads is growing.

Russ Crupnick, an analyst at consumer research group NPD, said the number of U.S. households engaged in P2P over the last year rose 7 percent, while the number of illegal downloads were up by 24 percent.

"P2P remains an unacceptable problem," said Mitch Bainwol, president of the Recording Industry Association of America. "The folks engaged in the practice are doing more of it.

The Recording Industry Association of America (RIAA) succeeded in closing some companies behind file-swapping, such as Grokster and Kazaa, starting in 2005.

But shutting down the companies that marketed the applications does not always kill the network.

"If you've got the software you can still file-share. The rulings just means you can't distribute (the software) anymore," said Wayne Rosso, a former chief executive of Grokster.

Pirates as Partners

In the last year, the music industry's focus has been on more high profile Web sites like News Corp.'s social networking site MySpace and YouTube, Google Inc.'s online video sharing site.

French media group Vivendi's Universal Music Group, along with fellow record companies Warner Music Group and Sony BMG, have signed revenue-sharing agreements with YouTube to let its users legally distribute their music on the site.

Universal Music Group also sued MySpace last year for letting users distribute its artists' works, a case that Universal says it expects to end in a settlement.

The record companies are now partners with "what they used to call pirates," Rosso said. The reason is that a company like YouTube has tens of millions of young music fans that music companies want to sell to.

"The record labels are saying on the one hand it's piracy so we've got to provide protection," said Jon Diamond, chief executive of ArtistDirect. "But on the other hand, it's their audience and they want to figure out ways to monetize that audience."

ArtistDirect's MediaDefender targets users of P2P networks and redirects them to video commercials when they search for files to swap illegally.

Stopping All Illegal Downloading Doesn't Guarantee More Sales

Even if record companies could eradicate all illegal downloading, there is no guarantee that people who swap songs for free would actually switch to buying music legally.

But the industry's strategy is to slow down P2P sharing and hope that legal digital music sales will eventually make up the shortfall.

"Obviously it's been a huge impediment to the growth of the legal market," said Larry Kenswil, Universal Music's top digital executive.

"But the growth of the legal market has been spectacular, he said. "P2P is not going to go away but the relative problem will drop for us.

SEVEN

Digital Music Gains Importance in the Music Industry

International Federation of the Phonographic Industry

> In the following viewpoint the International Federation of the Phonographic Industry (IFPI) states that legal purchases of digital music are becoming more important to the recording industry. The growth is attributed to a variety of things, including legal actions against large-scale P2P (person to person) uploaders, as well as combining digital technology with its traditional skills in bringing music to consumers. The big winners in the increase of the importance of digital music are consumers, who now have access to 24-hour a day online store shelves. IFPI is a worldwide organization, with its membership comprising some 1400 record companies in around 70 countries.

- Digital music sales estimated to double to around US$2 billion in 2006
- Single track downloads estimated up 89% at 795 million
- Available tracks double to four million, via 500 online services in over 40 countries worldwide
- Portable music players help drive digital music consumption
- New revenue streams and business models emerge
- Lawsuits impact illegal file-sharing, but "gatekeeper" ISPs must act to curb digital piracy

Music downloads offer consumers more choices than ever before, including 24-hour access and "shelves" that never need to be stocked.

Statistics on Digital Sales Show Increases

Record labels have become digitally literate companies, selling an estimated US$2 billion worth of music online or through mobile phones in 2006 (trade revenues), almost doubling the market in the last year.

Digital sales now account for around 10% of the music market as record companies experiment and innovate with an array of business models and digital music products, involving hundreds of licensing partners.

Among new developments in 2006, the number of songs available online doubled to four million, thousands of albums were released across many digital formats and platforms, classical music saw a "digital dividend" and advertising-funded services became a revenue stream for record companies.

However, despite this success, digital music has not yet achieved the "holy grail" of compensating for the decline in CD sales. Meanwhile, digital piracy and the devaluation of music content are a real threat to the emerging digital music business.

Research suggests legal actions against large-scale P2P [peer-to-peer] uploaders—some 10,000 of which were announced in 18 countries in 2006—have helped contain piracy, reducing the proportion of internet users frequently file-sharing in key European markets. Yet actions against individual uploaders are only the second best way of dealing with the problem. IFPI [International Federation of the Phonographic Industry] is stepping up its campaign for action from ISPs [Internet Service Providers] and will take whatever legal steps are necessary.

The conclusions are published today in IFPI's Digital Music Report 2007, a comprehensive round-up of developments in the sector.

IFPI's report shows how the record industry is combining digital technology with its traditional skills of discovering and marketing music. It also sets out where the music sector needs action by government and its industry partners to tackle piracy and prevent the undermining of its intellectual property rights.

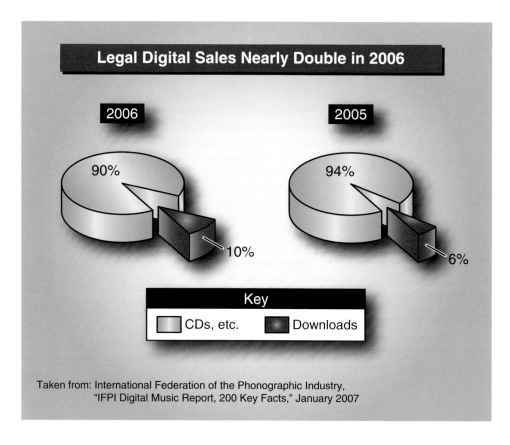

Legal Digital Sales Nearly Double in 2006

2006

90%

10%

2005

94%

6%

Key

CDs, etc.   Downloads

Taken from: International Federation of the Phonographic Industry, "IFPI Digital Music Report, 200 Key Facts," January 2007

Digital Is Empowering the Music Consumer

Consumers are finding that digital technology is helping to change their purchasing habits. They are taking advantage of the unlimited 'shelf space' in online stores, buying recordings that would have long vanished from the shelves of even the largest offline stores.

Recent months have also seen digital music distribution channels diversify. A-la-carte download services, led by iTunes, remain the dominant digital format, but they compete in a mixed economy with subscription services, mobile mastertones and more recently new advertising-supported models and video licensing deals on sites like YouTube and MySpace.

Mobile music accounted for about half of global digital revenues in 2006, but the split between mobile and online varies sharply by country. In Japan around 90% of digital music sales are accounted for by mobile purchases. 2007 could prove to be a landmark year in the mobile music market, as handset makers such as Nokia and Sony Ericsson develop their music phone series. Meanwhile, Apple has announced the launch of the much anticipated iPhone.

Portable players are one of the major drivers of growth in the digital sector. New figures show that the proportion of portable player owners who source mainly from paid downloads is roughly the same as the proportion who source mainly from unauthorised P2P and free websites (14%). Yet there is still concern at the relatively low levels of digitally purchased music that is stored on devices.

Digital Piracy Is Still a Massive Problem

There is mixed news for the industry when it comes to digital piracy. Independent research analysts Jupiter suggest that record number of high-profile lawsuits against large-scale uploaders in 2006 did have a deterrent effect on illegal file-sharers. As broadband penetration across Europe doubled to 40% between 2004 and 2006, the proportion of users regularly file-sharing fell from 18% to 14%. In the US, lawsuits were the most cited reason by computer users for changing from unauthorised P2P to legal downloading.

Key successes against illegal operators were recorded in 2006; including Kazaa in Australia, Bearshare in the US, ZoekMP3 in Netherlands and Kuro in Taiwan.

Yet digital piracy is still a massive problem for the music industry and one of the major reasons that the surging legitimate digital market is not expected to make up the shortfall in the decline of the physical market in 2006.

Record Industry Has Evolved to Think Digitally

IFPI Chairman and CEO John Kennedy said: "The record industry today has evolved into a digital thinking, digitally literate business. Revenues in 2006 doubled to about $2 billion and by 2010 we expect at least one quarter of all music sales worldwide to be digital. This is a market combining evolution and revolution, where the learning curve is changing direction on a regular basis.

"The chief winners in the rise of digital music are consumers. They have effectively been given access to 24-hour music stores with unlimited shelf space. They can consume music in new ways and formats—an iTunes download, a video on YouTube, a ringtone or a subscription library.

"Yet the market remains a challenge. Other industries, such as film and newspapers, are struggling with the same problems that we have had to live with. As an industry we are enforcing our rights decisively in the fight against piracy and this will continue. However, we should not be doing this job alone. With cooperation from ISPs we could make huge strides in tackling internet piracy globally. It is very unfortunate that it seems to need pressure from governments or even action in the courts to achieve this, but as an industry we are determined to see this campaign through to the end."

EIGHT

MySpace Helps Performers by Connecting Musicians and Fans

Josh Belzman

> In the following viewpoint Josh Belzman gives the reasons why MySpace, and other social networking sites, are good for musicians. MySpace has become a pop icon since its debut in the fall of 2003. While developers didn't set out to develop a music powerhouse, that's what it has become to musicians. Bands, both new and established, use MySpace as a promotional tool. It is particularly useful for small bands, who can make a name for themselves and their music, without the time and money involved in promotion in the face to face world. Josh Belzman is a writer and producer with MSNBC.com.

Looking for a new band to call your own, or hoping to turn weekend jam sessions into a career?

Thanks to the emergence of MySpace.com and other social networking sites, the Web is becoming a giant audition stage where millions of fans lay in wait.

From weekend hacks to Grammy-winning acts, more than 600,000 bands are using MySpace to upload songs and videos, announce shows, promote albums and interact with fans.

Josh Belzman, "Bands, Fans Sing New Tune on MySpace," MSNBC.com, February 13, 2006. Republished with permission of MSNBC, conveyed through Copyright Clearance Center, Inc.

"Bands are going to MySpace because it's free and they don't have to know how to do a Web site," said Tom Anderson, the site's 29-year-old co-founder and president. "But the biggest reason is because there are 43 million people on MySpace."

The site's astronomic growth since its fall 2003 launch—it's adding 4 million users a month—has made MySpace a pop icon and a corporate darling. Last summer, media mogul Rupert Murdoch paid $580 million to acquire the site and its parent company, Intermix. MySpace has become the third most visited Web domain (Google is No. 1), started its own record label and premiered new releases by several high-profile artists, including Madonna, Neil Diamond and Nine Inch Nails.

"Every day it seems we hit these new milestones," Anderson said.

This Community is Clickable

Anderson didn't set out to create a music powerhouse. MySpace was conceived as a cyber community where people in the same city or on opposite ends of the Earth could meet and correspond—"a place for friends." Anderson, a fan of independent bands, said he also recognized that the site could bridge the gap between musicians and fans.

"Part of the appeal (of MySpace) is that people aren't here just for music, but casual fans can find it here," Anderson said. "Bands themselves can reach out and find fans. It's really opened up opportunities for bands to promote themselves."

MySpace Music is the prime convergence point for bands and fans. Users can search for artists by name, genre, location or keyword. The section promotes new and well-established acts through exclusive content such as streaming audio and video. Audioslave, Weezer, Depeche Mode and other artists have previewed entire albums on the site ahead of their official release.

What sets MySpace and rival sites such as Friendster, TagWorld and Pure Volume apart from music giants MTV.com and Rollingstone.com is a blend of inclusiveness and interconnectivity. Any and all artists are welcome on MySpace, from Christian artists to death metal thrashers, and everything on the site is linked to something else. Click on a user's image and you're sent to a profile featuring pictures, blogs, personal interests and links to cyber pals and bands. Keep clicking and you're sent to more profiles and search results. Bands can post concert listings, interact with MySpace users and make songs available for download or background music.

"Social networking is one of the best examples of what the Web can do: connect people, whether it's at the micro level or the macro level, one-to-one or hundreds of thousands of people at once," said Toby Lewis, editorial director at London-based Music Ally.

Bands frequently use MySpace to keep fans informed of performance dates and new releases of their music.

DIY Promotional Tool

Jonathan Buck, guitarist and lead singer for the Brooklyn indie rock group Coppermine, says his band's profile on MySpace has drawn nearly 300,000 visitors. The band can instantly distribute messages and news to more than 115,000 MySpace users who have added Coppermine as a "friend" on their profile. Thanks to the broad reach of MySpace, Coppermine no longer has to flood radio stations with CDs or plaster concert posters around town.

"A MySpace profile is so efficient and so effective that it supplants a lot of that other stuff," Buck said.

Likening MySpace to a big music festival, Buck says the site allows small bands to make a name for themselves without spending time and money on the menial tasks usually associated with band development.

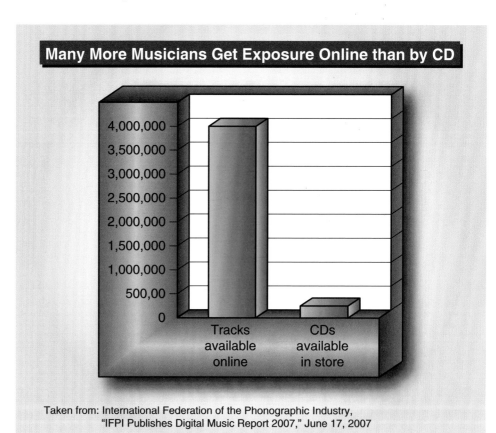

Taken from: International Federation of the Phonographic Industry, "IFPI Publishes Digital Music Report 2007," June 17, 2007

"You go to a big rock show where a big band is headlining— say, Audioslave—and you're there with CDs and posters, waiting in the rain to hand this stuff out to the crowd after the show. MySpace allows you to do that everyday, without spending any money," he said.

Coppermine's fans aren't the only ones following the band online. Buck said the band has been contacted by managers, promoters, music labels, Webzines, DJs and others "who definitely wouldn't have heard us if not for MySpace."

The site's been a boon to music fans, as well

"I mainly use the music section in MySpace to look for up-and-coming bands," said Nate Yeakel, or "MastaNate," as the 31-year-old Southern Californian punk fan is know to his friends on MySpace. "I've seen links to even the smallest of bands' MySpace pages. When there, you can usually find a link to either their merchandise or their label support, which can also turn you onto more bands.

"I guess the best way to describe MySpace is that it proves the 'Six Degrees of Separation' theory."

A Place for the Big Boys

Signed bands that already have a large fan base and the marketing power of a record label have also been drawn in by the DIY appeal of MySpace.

"It's this great new place for instant gratification," said Chris Carrabba, lead singer and songwriter for the rock band Dashboard Confessional, which is signed with Vagrant Records.

Carrabba logged onto MySpace for the same reason Anderson created the site: to connect with friends. Carrabba, who spends much of his time touring, said the site provides a central meeting place, anonymity, and a chance to connect with new fans.

"We've become a fairly popular band, especially among Web-savvy kids," Carrabba said. "I do believe that's what made us. But there are plenty of people that haven't heard of us, or heard us yet."

Dashboard Confessional's nearly 169,000 online fans have translated into concert patrons, as Carrabba found out when his band performed at a special concert in Los Angeles in October commemorating the second anniversary of MySpace.

"The MySpace anniversary party was kind of a reunion between bands, and probably the same thing for 'civilians' on MySpace," he said. "You had people from everywhere there."

Branching Beyond Cyberspace

The L.A. concert also coincided with MySpace's latest music venture, a new record label. The site has partnered with Interscope Records to form a label featuring both well-established and breakthrough acts. A MySpace Records compilation album released last fall put the music from more than a dozen bands, including Dashboard Confessional, into the hands of millions of consumers.

"Honestly it's just something I wanted to do," Anderson said of the label. "It seemed like a fun way to support bands. It's not a huge part of the business. It's a completely separate venture and in no way will it affect what we do with bands and labels. Maybe we'll sign three or four bands a year."

While MySpace Records might be seen as an extension of Anderson's affinity for indie music, his site has become its own animal. Murdoch's acquisition of MySpace is evidence that major media companies are more than willing to throw big money at sites to "test the waters and see what they can do," music analyst Lewis said. At the same time, record labels that have relied on traditional promotion schemes—radio play, street teams and magazine write-ups—are also wading into new Web waters.

"Labels understand people are spending more time online than on other mediums. Radio is more constrained. MTV is down to about 10 videos a day," said MySpace CEO Chris DeWolfe. "MySpace has become the place for awareness of new music and exclusive content. We can point music out ahead of its official release in a very organic way."

Last year, Nine Inch Nails, Beck and Queens of the Stone Age each enjoyed their biggest-ever album releases, according to Interscope. The albums were featured prominently on MySpace and streaming previews were available on the site days before they hit store shelves.

Catching Fire or Bound to Fail?

DeWolfe maintains that even more rewarding than major acts finding success on MySpace, is that the site is removing some of the traditional barriers that have confronted up-and-coming artists.

"Big labels in the past were the gatekeepers that would allow a band to make a living or not, but labels are signing fewer bands," he said. "Along with new production tools, MySpace allows a band to reach 43 million people. It allows a band to make a living and to fill up shows."

Lewis sounds a cautious note over the potential for MySpace or other social networking sites to revolutionize the music landscape. Online trends can arrive with a flourish only to fade into obscurity, he said.

"I'm not convinced (media companies) know how they're going to make use of these sites. It's really anyone's guess how the new world and the old world will come together," he said. "We're hearing stories of people being paid to stay up all night and add friends to a band's MySpace page. There's a potential for it to burn out if it's not managed correctly."

Ultimately, social networking sites may be a boon to investors even if they fail to directly impact record or concert sales. The key, Lewis said, is online advertising and the data-mining potential offered by MySpace and its rivals.

"Almost without thinking about it, people put their entire biography on their MySpace page—their favorite bands, their likes and dislikes," he said.

Media companies will have to be careful how they use such information, Lewis cautioned.

"It could go wrong if it starts to be abused by record labels and marketers."

It may be hard to put the genie back in the bottle. New users are flocking to MySpace every day and Internet surfers expect to find bands on the site. Some bands have stopped promoting their own Web sites in favor of a MySpace profile. Some, like Coppermine and Dashboard Confessional, maintain a presence across multiple Web communities. Both musicians Buck and Carrabba said MySpace has become a key piece of their bands' promotional ensemble.

"It's absolutely a great tool," Buck said. "Any kind of band out there that is trying to get something done is using MySpace.

NINE

MySpace Harms Performers by Encouraging Copyright Infringement

Chris Morris and Carl DiOrio

In the following viewpoint Chris Morris and Carl DiOrio provide quotes from Universal Music Group (UMG) and MySpace that outline how MySpace harms performers by the way it currently claims no responsibility for what its members file-share. UMG maintains Myspace knows and simply ignores the fact that members are posting user-stolen intellectual property belonging to others. MySpace indicates it doesn't encourage or condone copyright violation, so it is not responsible for what is posted. They maintain they are in full compliance with the Digital Millennium Copyright Act. Chris Morris and Carl DiOrio are writers with the Hollywood Reporter. which has been covering the entertainment industry for more than seventy-five years.

Universal Music Group and its publishing companies have sued MySpace and its parent company News Corp., alleging that the wildly popular site facilitates and encourages "rampant" infringement of thousands of UMG's copyrights.

Chris Morris and Carl DiOrio, "Universal Music Sues MySpace over Copyrights," HollywoodReporter.com, November 18, 2006. Reproduced by permission.

The action, filed Friday in federal court in Los Angeles, seeks maximum statutory damages of $150,000 for each copyrighted work infringed either directly or indirectly and an injunction barring further infringing acts.

Users Steal Content to Post on MySpace

Said UMG in its suit: "The foundation of MySpace is its so-called 'user-generated content.' However, much of that content is not 'user-generated' at all. Rather, it is the 'user-stolen' intellectual property of others, and MySpace is a willing partner in that theft."

MySpace has been accused of fostering copyright infringement by refusing to restrict its users' ability to illegally post music on the site.

The action continues, "Notwithstanding MySpace's frank admission that it is 'unable,' i.e., prohibited by law, from offering its music and video services without first obtaining the permission of the copyright owner, MySpace has knowingly and intentionally operated its business on the fiction that it has obtained the licenses it needs from members that MySpace well knows are not the true copyright owners.

"MySpace harbors no illusion that the countless MySpace members who have posted these bootleg videos and pirated sound records to MySpace have done so lawfully. MySpace simply ignores its own admonition in its terms of use about first obtaining the permission of the copyright owner."

The suit cites U2, 50 Cent, the Black Eyed Peas, Mariah Carey, the Killers, No Doubt, Kanye West and Prince among dozens of acts whose recordings or compositions have allegedly been pirated on the site, which is described in the complaint as "a vast virtual warehouse for pirated copies of music videos and songs."

UMG notes that rapper Jay-Z's much-anticipated album, "Kingdom Come,". . . already is "widely available for streaming and downloading on MySpace."

In a separate statement, UMG said: "Businesses that seek to trade off on our content and the hard work of our artists and songwriters shouldn't be free to do so without permission and without fairly compensating the content creators."

UMG—whose chairman and CEO Doug Morris has been outspoken about his intention to protect the company's music against online infringers—filed suit in October against peer-to-peer sites Grouper.com and Bolt.com, seeking similar damages.

MySpace Creates a Tool for Copyright Holders

The UMG suit against MySpace was filed almost simultaneously with an announcement from the site that it planned to launch a tool that will make it easier and faster for copyright holders to remove content they allege is unauthorized.

The tool—currently being tested with Fox and MLB Advanced Media—will allow copyright holders to digitally flag any user-posted video containing content that they own and allege is unauthorized. MySpace would then remove any of the flagged videos.

MySpace recently announced a licensing deal with Gracenote implementing fingerprinting technology that would bar the posting of unauthorized music on the site. . . .

MySpace Claims They're Not Responsible

A statement from MySpace about the UMG suit said in part: "We have been keeping UMG closely apprised of our industry-leading efforts to protect creators' rights, and it's unfortunate they decided to file this unnecessary and meritless litigation. We provide users with tools to share their own work—we do not induce, encourage or condone copyright violation in any way.

"We are in full compliance with the Digital Millennium Copyright Act and have no doubt we will prevail in court. Moreover, we proactively take steps to filter unauthorized music sound recordings and have implemented audio fingerprinting technology. We will continue working to be the gold standard in protecting creators' rights as well as the world's leading lifestyle portal."

Several defendants in previous copyright-infringement suits have failed in attempts to shield themselves with the DMCA's so-called safe-harbor provision, which applies in situations involving the mere hosting of Web site material. The UMG suit claims that MySpace also reformats material "uploaded by their users in order to facilitate the further copying and distribution of such works to and by as many users as possible."

Ever since the U.S. Supreme Court sided with the studio in [2005] MGM v. Grokster decision, it's considered scant defense to claim that a site also engages in the swapping of legal materials. But it could bear watching if MySpace uses its planned copyright-protection tool as a defense in the UMG suit.

"One question is whether it is sufficient to make the tool available to the content owner and make the content owner responsible to police the site," said Jeffrey Liebenson, an intellectual property attorney with the New York law firm of Herrick, Feinstein. "One of the raging controversies is whether the obligation to monitor infringing content is the responsibility of the content owner or the online user."

The matter also is at the heart of pending litigation involving some book publishers and the Google search site, Liebenson noted. Yet for all the technical arguments at the heart of the dispute, a judge could end up ruling on the UMG suit based on more simple fairness issues, he added.

"The Grokster case was a really good example of the Supreme Court using common sense and not getting all wrapped up in technicalities," Liebenson said. "They said there's something intrinsically offensive about what (Grokster) was doing."

TEN

Netlabels and Creative Commons Licensing Offer a Solution for Digital Music

Bjorn Hartmann

In the following viewpoint Bjorn Hartmann asserts that the use of netlabels, also called online labels, web labels, or MP3 labels, used to distribute music in digital audio formats, such as MP3s, can work with Creative Commons Licensing to solve many of the problems in the music industry for artists, producers, and consumers. Netlabels, unlike traditional recording labels or companies, blurs the distinction between producers and listeners, since the means of production are available to nearly anyone with a computer. Bjorn Hartmann has been involved in the international electronic music industry for over a decade. In 2003 he launched the netlabel textone.org, which introduced established recording artists to free online publishing using Creative Commons licenses.

Before internet access was widely available and before recording technology became affordable to home users, groups of young computer buffs exchanged their musical creations using a network of dial-in bulletin board systems. Their pieces were written using *tracker* software that offered simple arrangement and effects processing capabilities for a limited number of sample based instruments. Constraints of computing power imposed a distinct low-fidelity aesthetic on most productions. Interestingly, the music files that were exchanged were "open source" in that each file exposed its musical source code—the complete sequencing information as well as any sound samples employed—to the public for inspection and reuse. No one involved made a living off of tracked music; but a distinct sense of community arose which led to a series of Europe-wide meetings for competitions between groups. Perhaps because the lack of financial stakes, the scene never adopted a restrictive licensing model—sharing and re-use of music were considered basic principles of the community.

Netlabels: a New Model for Free Creative Commons-based Online Distribution

Recently, more and more traditional musicians realized what the tracker scene had presciently grasped many years before: if the goal is to share your creation with others and if musical information can be efficiently delivered as just data—why not jettison the carrier media? Moreover, if for small labels the dysfunctions of the independent music industry are largely attributable to the cost of handling the carrier media, would a digital distribution method not improve their lot? For the DJ attached to the standard tools of his craft, workarounds like Final Scratch that enable the use of physical interfaces to play back digital files are now readily available. What reasons remain to keep the carriers other than an innate human tendency to collect and hoard tangible objects? The shift away from identifying music with commodity products and towards a community-interaction based framework closely aligned forward-thinking artists with the principles of Creative Commons. Loosely translating the filtering and aggregating functions of traditional labels, but eschewing a commercial model, the term *netlabel* was coined to circumscribe these artist groups' activities.

A quasi-standard for operating netlabels has crystallized in the meantime. Most netlabels offer high-quality downloads in MP3 or OGG format from their websites, which also feature extensive information about the contributing artists with links to other related projects. Discussion forums and message boards for an open exchange about the music are common. Downloads are free of charge and labels explicitly allow for non-commercial copying of their material, mostly through the Creative Commons *no derivatives, non-commercial, attribution* license, recently recast as the *music sharing* license. Digital library sites such as *archive.org* and *scene.org* donate unlimited storage space and bandwidth to the projects, thus significantly reducing the hosting cost for netlabel operators.

While this general model has been adopted by many labels, it must be added that it is by no means normative. Because of the relative absence of economic pressures, a wide variety of approaches are viable. Some netlabels are explicitly rejecting associations with the commercial music world; others see net audio as a stepping stone to enter the traditional industry, while still other straddle the boundary. Some netlabels have ideological goals cast into manifestoes; others just enjoy sharing their work without financial burdens. This diversity has led some to complain about the wildly differing quality of material offered. In return, specialized online magazines covering netlabels such as Moritz Sauer's *Phlow* have begun to take on an editorial role, surveying the wide field and picking out gems. At least one national print music magazine, the German *de:bug*, regularly features articles about netlabels. No other literature exists on netlabels, but they have recently become a topic of discussion at academic and professional conferences such as *Freebitflows, Wizards of OS,* or the *mem Congress.* Next, the precise nature of the affinity between netlabels and the Creative Commons project will be described.

Four Reasons Why Netlabels Have Adopted Creative Commons Licensing

There are four major reasons why the free, non-commercial licensing scheme represented by the Creative Commons *music sharing* license is attractive for artists, netlabel owners and audiences. Each will be discussed in turn below.

• Reason #1: Promotion

Promotion is the most direct and self-serving motive for an artist: releasing music online and allowing listeners to share that music with others has to make sense for the producer, otherwise the model will not find widespread use. For independent niche music it does make sense. . . . One can actually reach a larger audience by publishing works online for free than by using traditional channels. Listeners are more likely to seek out new material if this comes at no cost to them and they will share the music with others if they are actively encouraged to pass the music on via file sharing networks, on CD, or however else they desire. Creative Commons licensed music then has the potential to enjoy both wider and faster diffusion. . . .

• Reason #2: Freedom from economic pressures

Non-commercial distribution enables widespread availability of music with limited commercial appeal. Economic considerations prevent much experimental/niche-audience music from being published on physical sound carriers at all. Of the existing releases, many are manufactured at a financial loss—an arrangement that is hardly ideal for producers or consumers. Producers simply cannot afford sub-breakeven releases over the long run. For consumers, copies of these limited releases are hard (if not impossible) to come by if they missed a record's initial release or if they are not blessed with access to a specialty shop carrying said items. Because no physical distribution channel is needed, audiences everywhere can enjoy Creative Commons licensed online music. . . .

• Reason #3: Community building

Communities live and die by the interaction between their members. Innovation is facilitated by having a sense of what already exists. Creativity in general never arises out of a void—it always incorporates prior experience and exposure. To build a vibrant, innovative, creative music scene requires fostering interaction with each other and encouragement of artistic exchange. Creative Commons licenses construct a positive, conducive environment for doing so. To clarify this point, one can contrast the netlabel

Netlabels provide an inexpensive way for musical artists to share their work and acquire fans beyond their local communities.

scene with the mainstream music market: netlabels are not interested in creating the kind of artificial distinction between producers and consumers that is promoted by the major labels. Netlabels are not interested in building one-way pipelines that push out products conceived by the marketing departments down to the masses. In electronic music, where the means of production are available to nearly anyone with a computer, each listener is also likely to turn into a producer. The distribution system for such a kind of music should reflect this equiposition of artists and audiences. By building a system based on respect and trust rather than intimidation and litigation, a fair and open licensing scheme such as Creative Commons creates the positive base for future interaction.

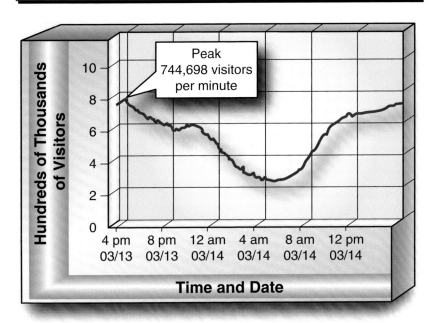

Taken from: Akamai Net Usage Index

• Reason #4: Future-proofing

How many of today's netlabels will still be around in five years? Hopefully a sizeable number, but almost certainly not all of them. How about in fifteen years? Or in fifty? The independent market has always been characterized by a high fluctuation rate brought about by economic pressures. One should therefore already think today about what will happen to today's music tomorrow, when particular artists or labels are no longer around. Art always arises from the history of prior creations, so the community should be interested in making sure that future generations have full access to the music that is created right now. Creative Commons licenses ensure that this happens. Many works published under the restrictive traditional copyright regime are in danger of being "orphaned" for an obscenely long time if the exclusive copyright holder dies or disappears. Without a legal way of distributing and sharing these works, most vanish from the public's collective memory for so long that they are unlikely to be resurrected after they pass into the public domain. In contrast, any work released under a Creative Commons license that allows for non-commercial distribution is more likely to survive since any single copy can legally spawn a future "re-release." As long as some user somewhere still has one copy of a Creative Commons work, the art is not lost—no matter if the artist is still around or not. Long term digital library initiatives like the Internet Archive increase the chances of a transmission of today's work through time. Thus, a sense of history and continuity is created and the future is not deprived of the achievements of today.

ELEVEN

Advertising Revenue is the Answer to Music Piracy

Louis Hau

> In the following viewpoint Louis Hau interviews Ruckus President and Chief Executive, Michael Bebel, on the launch of a free ad-supported nationwide service for music downloads. The service targets U.S. college students, who are in the age group shown to be the most likely to download music from unauthorized peer-to-peer (p2p) web sites. National advertisers have responded positively to the project, mainly in response to the licensing deals Ruckus made with all four major record labels to provide their music. Despite the restriction that the tree downloads must be used on a PC, not a portable music player, Bebel maintains that the Ruckus service will help switch young people to legitimate services. Louis Hau is a media writer for Forbes.com.

A Free Ad-supported Music Download Service Goes Nationwide

Ruckus was founded in 2003 by a couple of MBA candidates at the Massachusetts Institute of Technology and currently serves 82 U.S. colleges and universities. The Herndon, Va., company's partner institutions range from small schools you've never heard of to big ones like the University of Southern California, Michigan State University, the University of North Carolina at Chapel Hill, the Georgia Institute of Technology and Princeton University.

Ruckus Targets Those Most Likely to Download Illegal Music

Today, Ruckus is opening up its service to any U.S. college student with a valid .edu e-mail address. It's a big step for a company that has quietly garnered a base of users who happen to occupy the demographic most likely to otherwise download music from unauthorized peer-to-peer sites.

Software engineers process CDs to stream online through Musicmatch's digital jukebox service. Subscribers can pay to download and keep songs they like.

That audience is no doubt one of the reasons why Ruckus has managed to beat SpiralFrog and other developing download services in locking up licensing deals with all four major record labels—Universal Music Group, Sony BMG Music Entertainment, Warner Music Group and EMI Music—as well as a host of independent labels.

That selection and Ruckus' growing customer base have, in turn, helped draw national advertisers, including AT&T, JPMorgan Chase's Chase Bank, Barnes & Noble and Morgan Stanley's Discover Card.

Ruckus President and Chief Executive Michael Bebel joined the company last July, five months after its basic download-to-PC service switched to a free, ad-supported business model from its original incarnation as a subscription service.

"The big appeal for me was in looking at what happened when they flipped to the ad-supported model," Bebel says. "Instantly, they had great response from both the universities and the students. The update and penetration rates were incredible. . . . It was evident that this thing had traction that nobody else had achieved."

Bebel is a former president and chief operating officer of Napster and came to Ruckus from Mashboxx, a yet-to-launch music download service where he was president and chief executive. (What's the hold up at Mashboxx? "They have a lot to take on to get to the marketplace," is all Bebel will say.)

Ruckus Downloads Are Only for PC Use

Ruckus claims to have more than 300,000 registered users, but whether it will prove to be a big hit among college students nationwide isn't yet clear. Most students who download music have grown accustomed to getting tunes from unauthorized file-sharing networks. While such services can sometimes pass on viruses and spyware, users can do whatever they want with the downloads—play them on their Apple iPods, burn them onto CDs for their friends, etc.

By contrast, Ruckus' downloads feature restrictions that are similar to those found on subscription services such as RealNetworks' Rhapsody, Napster and Yahoo! Music Unlimited. Users of Ruckus' free service can only download music tracks to their PC. The encrypted tracks, which are encoded in Microsoft's Windows Media Audio format, can't be burned to a CD and won't play on an iPod. For a $5 monthly fee, users can transfer downloaded tracks to a non-Apple MP3 player with PlaysForSure compatibility.

Bebel argues that Ruckus' growth is a sign that college students are willing to work within a restricted-use environment, particularly when it offers free access to music and an online community where users can view one another's playlists and share recommendations.

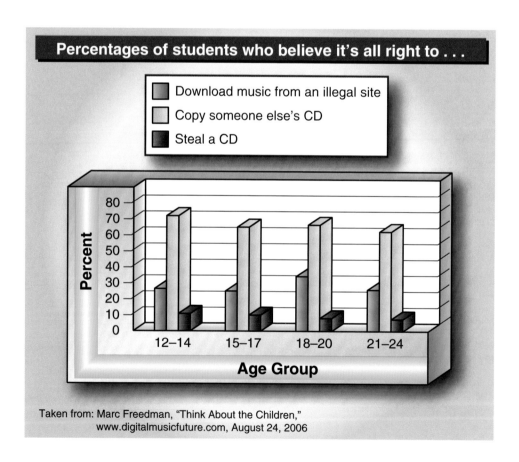

Percentages of students who believe it's all right to . . .

- Download music from an illegal site
- Copy someone else's CD
- Steal a CD

Taken from: Marc Freedman, "Think About the Children," www.digitalmusicfuture.com, August 24, 2006

"We're playing a role primarily as a discovery tool, where the world of music is available to these students with a community wrapped around it of their peers," he says.

Switching People to Legitimate Services

If any college student can now download music for free from Ruckus, where does that leave the company's partner colleges and universities, which either pay a fee to the company or agree to provide a minimum number of users? Because Ruckus sets up dedicated servers at its partner institutions, the schools save on the added bandwidth costs that would be incurred from students using the service, Bebel says. In addition, download speeds are greatly reduced.

Students at partner institutions can also sign up for a modest video download subscription service which costs $3 a month or $15 a semester. Subscribers can choose from a limited, rotating selection of about 4,000 movies and TV shows from General Electric's NBC Universal and Time Warner's Warner Bros. Entertainment, of which about 50 are usually available at any given time.

Mostly to hold on to students after they graduate, Ruckus offers alumni, faculty and staff with a valid .edu email address the option to subscribe to the service for $9 a month.

Bebel declines to say whether Ruckus is profitable, saying only that the service is "on track with our investors' expectations." Those investors include Battery Ventures, Eastward Capital, Pinnacle Ventures and Shelter Capital, which provided $13.7 million in a second round of financing last August.

"We're playing a role in combating piracy," he says. "If you can switch a young person to using a legitimate service like Ruckus, hopefully they're not going to use illicit services out there to obtain the content."

What You Should Know About Downloading Music

Facts About Downloading Music in the United States

- File-sharing software is legal, but downloading copyrighted music is illegal without the permission of the copyright holder.
- Civil liability can extend to the parents of under-age offenders, even if they were unaware that their child had been stealing copyrighted music. This means parents can be held financially liable for the cost of stolen music.
- The American Society of Composers, Authors, and Publishers (ASCAP) and iSAFE, a nonprofit foundation that teaches kids about Internet safety, launched an anti-piracy educational program in March of 2007 to visit schools across the United States.
- Record companies filed more than 18,000 music piracy lawsuits in United States courts up to the end of 2006.
- The music industry blames illegal file sharing of copyrighted music for a 23% worldwide decline in sales of music CDs between 2000 and 2006.
- Consumer research analysts noted a 7% rise in the number of American households engaged in filesharing in 2006, and a corresponding 24% increase in illegal downloads.
- In December 2006 report, Forrester Research said it did a strenuous, independent analysis of iTunes purchases and found that just 3.2% of all "online households," or homes that have computers and Internet connections, made an iTunes purchase over a one-year period.

- According to the Nielsen SoundScan data, CD sales in the US declined 20% in the first quarter of 2007 compared to same period in 2006. The change is attributed to such factors as increased digital sales and the closure of 800 music stores across the country.

- The online infringement of copyrighted music can be punished by up to 3 years in prison and $250,000 in fines. Repeat offenders can be imprisoned up to 6 years. Individuals also may be held civilly liable, regardless of whether the activity is for profit, for actual damages or lost profits, or for statutory damages up to $150,000 per infringed copyright.

- According to a 2006 survey by the Intellectual Property Institute at the University of Richmond's School of Law, more than half of all college students illegally download music and movies.

- According to Broadcast Music Inc., a performing-rights organization, ring-tone download music sales in the United States hit $600 million in 2006.

- On April 6, 2007, Apple Inc. announced it had sold 100 million iPods since launching the digital media player in November 2001.

- Music giant EMI (the world's 3rd largest music group) was the first to offer its vast music catalogue for download without special digital rights management (DRM) protection in April of 2007, allowing consumers to transfer songs between different types of digital players.

- On MySpace, the MyStores music ecommerce program launched Snocap in 2007, which allowed artists to sell MP3s directly from their profiles to members of the MySpace community, in order to increase access to paid downloads and eliminate illegal file sharing.

- The United States Fairness in Music Licensing Act of 1998 provides for a royalty originally set at 2%, paid by the first person who manufactures and distributes CDs labeled and sold for music use; it does not apply to blank computer CDs, even though they can be used to record music from the computer to CD. A similar royalty applies to stand-alone CD recorders, but not to CD burners used with computers.

Facts about International Music Downloads

- The International Federation of the Phonographic Industry (IFPI) predicted in 2006 that online sales would account for a quarter of all music sales worldwide by 2010.

- Worldwide sales of downloaded music, including cellphone ringtones, rose 82 percent to about $2 billion in 2006 to account for around 10 percent of music industry sales.

- Mobile music accounted for half of global digital music revenues in 2006, although its prominence varies by country, such as in Japan, where 90% of digital music sales are mobile purchases.

- Koreans are some of the most avid digital music consumers, with 51% of music sales there coming from digital sales during the first half of 2006.

- Analysts indicated that in 2006 the majority (83 percent) of European iPod owners did not regularly buy digital music. Just 17 percent of European iPod owners purchased digital music on an at least monthly basis.

- Increased file sharing of music in Canada coincided with a 42% ($558 million CDN dollars) decrease in annual retail sales of music between 1999 and 2005, which also meant a 20% loss in employment.

- Canadian artist Jully Black witnessed 2.8 million illegal file swapping requests for her music in the first two weeks of her album's release in 2005, compared with 15,000 copies sold of the same album.

- Canada imposes fees on recording mediums like blank CDs and similar items. These levies are used to fund musicians and song-writers for revenues lost due to consumer copying. The power to set rates and distribute the returns is vested in the Copyright Board of Canada.

- The three top countries downloading illegal music as identified by the International Intellectual Property Alliance in 2005 were: Russia, Mexico and Brazil. The estimated retail value of the pirated downloads was valued at: Russia—$475.9 million; Mexico—$376.5 million; and Brazil—$334.5 million.

- Officials in India seized pirated compact discs and cassettes worth 500 million rupees (US$11 million; euro8.24 million) in more than 10,000 raids across India between 2001 and 2006, and shut down more than 600 illegal Internet music sites.

- The International Federation of the Phonographic Industry (IFPI) said more than 1 billion music tracks were illegally downloaded in Brazil in 2005. Record company revenues in the country, the largest market in Latin America, fell from $724.7 million in 2000 to $394.2 million in 2005. The IFPI blamed the drop on illegal file sharing.

Facts about Downloading Music Laws & Actions Around the World

- In March, 2005, France's parliament voted against introducing the world's first blanket license for sharing digital media.
- In Canada, downloading copyright music from peer-to-peer file-sharing networks is legal, but uploading copyright protected files is not.
- A 2005 decision against the file-sharing company, Kazaa, in Australia, forced Kazaa to be responsible for and directly control the use of its software. This ruling did not make individuals responsible for illegal use of peer-to-peer file-sharing networks.
- In 2006 record companies sued and were granted settlements from the following file-sharing companies or networks: Allofmp3 .com in Russia, Zoekmp3 in the Netherlands, BearShare in the United States, and Kuro in Taiwan.
- Eleven music industry giants sued Yahoo! China in March 2007 for alleged copyright infringement, due to the number of searches conducted for pirated music files. The lawsuit was filed by the International Federation of the Phonographic Industry (IFPI) on behalf of their members, which included Warner Music, Sony BMG, EMI Group PLC and Universal Music Group.
- Members of European Union Legal Affairs' committee announced in March 2007 that criminal sanctions should only apply to those illegal file sharing infringements deliberately carried out to obtain a commercial advantage or make money. Piracy committed by private users for personal, non-profit purposes were excluded from the criminal sanctions.

- The International Federation of the Phonographic Industry (IFPI) and its member companies took legal action against more than 10,000 individuals who uploaded pirated music to peer-to-peer file sharing networks in 18 countries in 2006, including, for the first time, Brazil, Mexico, Poland and Portugal. The International Federation of the Phonographic Industry (IFPI) made a 2006 call to all governments to have Internet Service Providers (ISPs) take a greater role in stopping digital piracy. Many ISP contracts already make users agree that they will have their service cut off if they infringe on copyright legislations. IFPI would like governments to make this a part of all ISP contracts and enforce it.
- The European Union sent formal charges to Apple and the leading record companies in April of 2007, alleging they were restricting music sales in Europe by a policy that required consumers to only buy iTunes from online stores in their country of residence.
- The European Union of 27 countries created legislation expected to become law in the summer of 2007, which would introduce a maximum four-year prison sentence for intellectual property crimes, including music piracy, and fines of up to EUR91,050 ($121,430 USD), rising to EUR273,160 ($364,290 USD.) if organized crime involvement is proven. This legislation would replace widely diverse laws in place in the individual countries.
- Poor copyright control in South Africa resulted in the rampant spread of pirated music. Some estimates by the Recording Industry of South Africa put it at over 80 percent of available music, which left musicians living in poverty in 2006.

What You Should Do About Downloading Music

In 2003, a 12-year-old girl, Brianna LaHara, from New York, paid $29.99 for software that gave her access to online file-sharing services, so she could download music she enjoyed. Unfortunately, she was among the first to be sued by the record industry for sharing music over the Internet. That September her mother paid $2,000 to settle the lawsuit.

With 43% of 12,000 students in grades 5 through 12 who responded to a 2005–06 survey indicating they have downloaded music from the Internet, it is clear students need the facts about downloading music. The same survey indicated 58% of students admit to using the Internet unsafely, inappropriately, or illegally.

Following Downloading Music Laws

How do students follow the laws for downloading music? There are many legal sites to download music from that give part of the fee paid to the creators of the music—songwriters, musicians, and record companies. iTunes is the top source, followed by Real Music, Napster, eMusic, and MSN. Other companies are created regularly, so there will always be new sources to purchase music from, just as new music stores appear and disappear in the mall.

There are also online sources for free music available directly from bands and performers willing to share samples of their work. Many musicians make their start on the Internet community MySpace, as well as their own, or other smaller web sites, so they can be good sources for discovering new artists. Popular artists and bands often promote themselves online too, providing free videos or short song clips on their web sites.

Online music stores are also safe places to download music in other ways. Individuals sharing music in a file-sharing or peer-to-peer (p2p) network risk serious damage to their computers from malicious code. Officials claimed in 2004 that 45 percent of thousands of free files they collected via Kazaa, the most popular p2p client at the time, contained viruses, Trojan horses, and back doors. These types of codes can completely wipe out all of the information on a computer or do other types of damage to it.

Knowing What Is Legal

There are many ways students can break the law that they may be unaware of. First, like Brianna LaHara, students can become members of a file-sharing community or peer-to-peer network. While having file-sharing software is legal, downloading copyrighted music is illegal without the permission of the copyright holder in the United States. This means students cannot legally use the file-sharing software to access a download site where other people are the ones providing the content, instead of the owners of the music.

Some students misunderstand how the law works that lets them make MP3 copies of songs on specific blank CDs they've purchased (royalties have already been collected on these blanks). These copies are only intended as a back-up, just as all other computer data is backed up in case of a computer crash or hardware failure. Sharing this backup in any way is illegal: burning a CD for a friend; uploading the MP3 copy on the Internet, using a file-sharing network; or even attaching it in an email to a friend.

Emailing or sending an MP3 by instant messaging is against the law, because it creates an unauthorized copy and distributes someone else's creative work. A 2005-06 survey of 12,500 students in grades 5 through 12 indicated 48% of students believe they should have the unrestricted right to download music from the Internet. However, laws in the United States are in place to make sure music producers can make a living creating the music fans love to hear.

Understanding the Penalties
The United States "No Electronic Theft Law" (NET Act) outlines the penalties for copyright violations that involve illegal digital recordings:

- Criminal penalties can run up to three years in prison and/or $250,000 in fines, even if the theft was not committed for monetary or financial or commercial gain, for a first offense.
- If the music downloader expected something in return for providing the free music, even just swapping files, as in MP3 trading, he or she can be sentenced to as long as five years in prison.
- Regardless of whether the music downloader expected to profit, he or she is still liable in civil court for damages and lost profits of the copyright holder.
- Copyright holders can sue music downloaders directly for up to $150,000 in statutory damages for each of their copyrighted works illegally copied or distributed.

Some students believe that because they're underage, or younger than the legal age in their state, that the courts won't really do anything to them if they are caught downloading music illegally. In the United States civil liability can extend to the parents of under-age offenders, even if they were unaware that their child was stealing copyrighted music. This means parents can be held financially liable for the cost of stolen music, as Brianna LaHara's mother was.

Used unsafely and without regard for the laws, downloading music is a problem for everyone involved in the music industry, including fans. However, by following the laws and utilizing legal music download sites, fans can support the industry and help it grow.

American Society of Composers, Authors, & Publishers
One Lincoln Plaza
New York, NY 10023
(212) 621-6000 • Fax: (212) 724-9064
Web site: www.ascap.com

ASCAP is a membership association of more than 285,000 American composers, songwriters, lyricists, and music publishers of every kind of music. ASCAP protects the rights of its members by licensing and distributing royalties for the non-dramatic public performances of their copyrighted works.

Canadian Recording Industry Association
85 Mowat Avenue
Toronto, Ontario M6K 3E3
(416) 967-7272 • Fax: (416) 967-9415
Web site: www.cria.ca

The Canadian Recording Industry Association (CRIA) is a non-profit trade organization that was founded in 1964 to represent the interests of Canadian companies that create, manufacture and market sound recordings.

Creative Commons
543 Howard Street
5th Floor San Francisco, CA 94105-3013
(415) 946-3070 • Fax: (415) 946-3001
Web site: creativecommons.org

Creative Commons is an organization that values innovation and protection equally, and is working to offer creators a best-of-both-worlds way to protect their works while encouraging certain uses of them—to declare "some rights reserved."

Cyberethics for Kids
Web site: www.cybercrime.gov/rules/kidinternet.htm

Web site created by the Computer Crime & Intellectual Property
Section of the United States Department of Justice.

United States Department of Justice
10th & Constitution Ave., NW
Criminal Division, (Computer Crime & Intellectual Property
Section)
John C. Keeney Building, Suite 600
Washington, DC 20530
Office of Public Affairs (202) 514-2007

This Web site from the Department of Justice outlines the ethics
and laws of cyberspace, which people should be aware of before
surfing. Interactive scenarios show the results of making specific downloading decisions. There are also teacher lesson plans
available.

International Federation of the Phonographic Industry (IFPI)
IFPI Secretariat
54 Regent Street
London
W1B 5RE
United Kingdom
+44 (0)20 7878 7900 • Fax: +44 (0)20 7878 7950
Email: info@ifpi.org
Web site: www.ifpi.org

IFPI represents the recordings industry worldwide, with a membership comprising some 1400 record countries in around 70 countries. IFPI's mission is to promote the value of recorded music, safe-
guard the rights of record producers, and expand the commercial
uses of recorded music in all markets where its members operate.

Recording Industry Association of America
Web site: www.riaa.com

The RIAA is the trade association that represents the recording industry in the United States. It works to protect intellectual property rights worldwide and the First Amendment rights of artists; conduct consumer industry and technical research; and monitor and review state and federal laws, regulations and policies.

BIBLIOGRAPHY

Books

Patrick Burkart and Tom McCourt, *Digital Music Wars: Ownership and Control of the Celestial Jukebox.* Lanham, MD: Rowman & Littlefield Publishers, Inc., 2006.

Ty Cohen, *The New Music Industry: How to Use the Power of the Internet to Multiply Your Industry Exposure, Fan Base and Income Potential Online!* Platinum Millennium Publishing, 2006.

Otto D'Agnolo and Caesar Bach, *The Music Business is Burning Down—Thank God!* New Bern, NC: Trafford Publishing, 2005.

Steve Gordon, *The Future of the Music Business: How to Succeed with the New Digital Technologies,* Milwaukee, WI: Backbeat Books, 2005.

Sameer Hinduja, *Music Piracy and Crime Theory.* New York, NY: LFB Scholarly Publishing LLC, 2005.

Scott Kelby, *The iPod Book: Doing Cool Stuff with the iPod and the iTunes Music Store,* 2nd edition. Berkeley, CA: Peachpit Press, 2005.

Candice M. Kelsey, *Generation MySpace: Helping Your Teen Survive Online Adolescence.* New York, NY: Marlowe & Company, 2007.

Dave Kusek and Gerd Leonhard, *The Future of Music: Manifesto for the Digital Music Revolution.* Boston, MA: Berklee Press, 2005.

Conrad Mewton, *All You Need to Know About Music & the Internet Revolution,* London, ON: Sanctuary, 2005.

Donald S. Passman, *All You Need To Know About the Music Business: 6th Edition,* Northampton, MA: Free Press, 2006.

Periodicals

Antony Bruno, "Charting the Course: By Helping the Digital Market, Record Labels Could Help Themselves," *Billboard*, March 17, 2007.

Ted Cohen, "A P2P Proposal: Let's Find Out if It's About Free Music or a Great Experience," *Billboard*, March 31, 2007.

Dan Daley, "Managing the Music: Too Many Tracks and Too Little Time to Find Them?" *Studio Monthly*, March 2007.

The Economist, "Facing the Music; Death of the Record Store," January 20, 2007.

ExtremeTech.com, "Digital Music, Movie Piracy on the Rise," February 7, 2007.

Brian Garrity and Todd Martens, "Net Effects: Three Big Ways the Net Neutrality Debate Affects the Music Business," *Billboard*, April 7, 2007.

Chandra M. Hayslett, "Music Pirates Going Overboard! Artists Fight Back to Protect Their Livelihoods," *Black Enterprise*, Feb 2007.

Catherine Holahan, "Music Downloading's New Deal; Free File-Sharing Services Are Considering Ad-Supported Business Models—But First, They Need to Win Over Music Label Foes," *Business Week Online*, Oct 31, 2006.

Mathew Honan, "Find Free Music: Go Online for No-Cost, Legal Tunes," *Macworld*, April 2007.

New Media Age, "Will We Miss DRM Once It's Gone?" April 5, 2007.

PC Magazine Online, "MySpace 'MyStores' Tie Bands Closer to Community," March 15, 2007.

Personal Computer World, "In the Beginning, There Was Rhythm," December 5, 2006.

RCR Wireless News, "Jobs, RIAA Tit for Tat on DRM Underscores Fragmented Music Biz," February 12, 2007.

Web sites
Digital Freedom
E-mail: info@digitalfreedom.org
URL: www.digitalfreedom.org

Digital Freedom asserts that digital technologies should allow everyone the freedom to be artists, innovators, producers and creators; to listen, watch and participate wherever, whenever and however they choose.

What's the Download?
Web site: www.whatsthedownload.com
Web site created by The Recording Academy (Grammy awards)
The Recording Academy
3402 Pico Blvd.
Santa Monica, CA 90405
Phone: (310) 392-3777
Fax: (310) 399-3090

WhatsTheDownload.com is a Web site for music fans to learn about the issues, to hear artists' views on downloading, and to create a dialogue between music makers and music fans. The Recording Academy, who created the site, is the voice of more than 17,000 music makers, all of whom have very different viewpoints on issues affecting music. The purpose of the Web site is to ensure that all voices have an equal place in the debate.

Creative Commons
  Licensing, 74–80
Cross-marketing, 16
  See also Promotion
Cyberethics for Kids (organi-
  zation), 95

Dashboard Confessional
  (band), 65–66, 68
Data-mining, 67
De:bug (print magazine), 76
Denmark, legal actions in, 48
Depeche Mode (band), 62
Diamond, Neil, 62
Digital File Check (soft-
  ware), 47
Digital Millennium
  Copyright Act, 69, 72
Digital music
  importance of, 8–9, 23,
    55–60
  licensing, 26, 74–80
  sales, 44–45, 51–52, 55,
    57–59, 76, 87–88
Digital rights management
  tools, 24, 34, 47, 71–72, 87
DiOrio, Carl, 69
Distribution
  costs of, 26–27, 42
  Internet-based, 19–20, 28–
    35, 45, 58, 75–77, 79–80
Dixie Chicks, 37
Downhill Battle (organiza-
  tion), 28
Downloading music
  action steps, 90–93
  facts, 86–90

helps artists, 28–35
helps music industry, 11–17
hurts artists, 36–43, 88
hurts music industry, 12–13,
  14, 18–27, 44–54
illegal, 44–54, 71, 91–93
laws regarding, 91–92
legal sites, 23–24, 43–48,
  51, 54, 57–60, 80, 81–85
myths regarding, 19–27
statistics, 9–10, 20–21,
  44–46, 55, 86, 91
See also File-sharing; Peer-
  to-peer services (P2P);
  Piracy
DVDs, 9, 24

Economic pressures, 77, 80
Education, copyright, 47–48,
  86
Elliot, Missy, 38
EMI Music, 83, 87, 89
The Eminem Show (album),
  21
EMusic.com, 91
EMusic.com, 91
Europe
  downloading in, 45–46, 57,
    75
  legal actions in, 59, 89–90
  music sales, 21, 88
  *See also specific European
    countries*
Experimental music, 20, 77

Fairness in Music Licensing
  Act of 1998, 87

PICTURE CREDITS